INVISIBLE NORTH

Alexandra Shimo

INVISIBLE

NORTH

The Search for Answers on a Troubled Reserve

DUNDURN

TORONTO

Editor: Michael Melgaard
Design: Courtney Horner
Cover design: Laura Boyle
Front cover image: Kashechewan First Nation, © Kevin A. Sandberg
Printer: Webcom

Library and Archives Canada Cataloguing in Publication

Shimo, Alexandra, author
     Invisible north : the search for answers on a troubled
reserve / Alexandra Shimo.

Includes bibliographical references.
Issued in print and electronic formats.
ISBN 978-1-4597-2292-7 (paperback).--ISBN 978-1-4597-2293-4
(pdf).--ISBN 978-1-4597-2294-1 (epub)

     1. Kashechewan First Nation. 2. Indian reservations--
Ontario, Northern. 3. Indians of North America--Ontario, Northern--
Social conditions. I. Title.

E78.O5S55 2016   305.897'07131   C2016-903093-8
                                               C2016-903094-6

1   2   3   4   5   20   19   18   17   16

  Canada

We acknowledge the support of the **Canada Council for the Arts** and the **Ontario Arts Council** for our publishing program. We also acknowledge the financial support of the **Government of Canada** through the **Canada Book Fund** and **Livres Canada Books**, and the **Government of Ontario** through the **Ontario Book Publishing Tax Credit** and the **Ontario Media Development Corporation**.

Care has been taken to trace the ownership of copyright material used in this book. The author and the publisher welcome any information enabling them to rectify any references or credits in subsequent editions.
                                                                  — *J. Kirk Howard, President*

The publisher is not responsible for websites or their content unless they are owned by the publisher.

Printed and bound in Canada.

VISIT US AT
Dundurn.com | @dundurnpress | Facebook.com/dundurnpress | Pinterest.com/dundurnpress

Dundurn
3 Church Street, Suite 500
Toronto, Ontario, Canada
M5E 1M2

This book is for the people of Kashechewan.
And for Lia Grimanis who guided its creation.

History, despite its wrenching pain, cannot be unlived, but if faced with courage, need not be lived again.

— Maya Angelou

Canadian history as we have lived it [is] not the version of it that finds its way into Canadian textbooks.

— George Erasmus

Contents

Author's Note

This was supposed to be a book about the rumoured water scandal in the northern Ontario reserve of Kashechewan. That's what I promised my publisher. And various versions of those chapters exist, in earlier drafts, which are now probably on some landfill somewhere, a place where there are more birds than people, full of things mostly forgotten. Parts of this book cover that story. But only a sliver. In the writing, it soon became apparent that it was impossible to detail it without telling my own tale too, the story of the nearly four months that I spent on Kashechewan First Nation reserve starting in September 2010, then returning in the flooding seasons of 2011 and 2014. Even as a visitor and a non-Aboriginal person, it was impossible not to be swept up in the reality of living in an isolated northern community. It was an experience that I would not trade for the world, but like many experiences that shape us, it took a great personal toll. To understand and tell that story, I had to employ several tools of the trade: I sometimes had to rely on the vagaries of memories a few years old. I have also shifted the timelines and changed people's names and identifying details to protect their privacy. And they deserve a thank you. That the people of Kashechewan opened their homes, and allowed me to stay in their community was an act of unquestionable generosity that taught me much and changed me in ways that I am still comprehending, for which I am ever grateful.

Prologue

Sitting in a car on the dusty main road to Kashechewan First Nation reserve, the doctor had a strange feeling that she was being used. She looked out the window. What didn't sit right? The stray dogs running alongside the vehicle? The graffitied houses boarded up with plywood? Or the fact that this was supposed to be a national emergency, yet everyone, from the driver laughing as he pointed out the town's landmarks, to his assistant, who had amiably helped the doctor with her luggage, seemed to be moving with carefree ease.

Lindsay MacMillan was a 28-year-old doctor, originally from North Sydney, Nova Scotia. She had flown to Kashechewan from Moose Factory, Ontario, where she was doing a residency. She had been told by her supervisor that the purpose of the trip was to treat people with symptoms of E. coli. The bacteria was said to be in the water. She had read it in the papers. And over the next few weeks, in late October 2005, she would continue to read it in the media, even though she told everyone who would listen that she saw no symptoms of E. coli, that locals there had been happily drinking the tap water, and no one was getting sick.

With no evidence of the bacteria, she spent her time going door to door taking photos. Heartbreaking, really. There were toilets overflowing with feces. Children playing in rooms filled with dirty dishes and garbage. Kids sleeping on the floor during the day because there wasn't enough space for everyone at night. It haunted her, and still troubles her to this day.

And so, when her photos were later shown by Kashechewan's leaders to the national and international media to bolster their case, well, it didn't surprise her. Good for them, she thought. Despair pushes many to the extreme. Sometimes the truth will only get you so far.

Introduction

Troubled was a word often used to describe Kashechewan by the time I became aware of it. That was in October 2005. Back then I was working for the CBC as a producer on various current affairs shows in radio and television, and like many of its employees, moving between contracts. It was a piecemeal existence, with long hours and little stability, but one advantage was that I got to explore where my own curiosity took me, whether it was indigenous rights or near-death experiences. I thought of my job as a paid investigator through the terrain of news and ideas, eager to uncover those hidden conflicts and stories that propelled the news forward. I had planned to apply this same principle to Kashechewan but it was impossible, at least from Toronto. For when I went to research the reserve in my books on indigenous history, there was almost nothing there. One of the books — the *Handbook of North American Indians*, Volume VI — mentioned that it had some of the things that we normally associate with northern communities — a Hudson's Bay store and a local elementary school — but that was about it. It was as if the reserve had previously existed in a void, and had emerged from the silence of nothingness to full-blown crisis.

When I finally arrived in Kashechewan, or Kash as locals call it, five years later, I found that wasn't it, not at all, there was a lot more to it than meets the eye. I suppose that's true of any place; life is always fuller than what's written down on the page. But Kashechewan had a number of characteristics that silenced its stories. It was more than 1,000 kilometres away from Toronto, and the only way in was by plane. It had no cell phone service, and the Internet was often down. Few people listed themselves in the phone book. And it was on a First Nation reserve, which meant that it was difficult for its leaders to publicize what was really happening. That's not an isolated incident — it's true of many Aboriginal communities. Over the centuries there have been many Native leaders, such as Joseph Onasakenrat, Frederick Ogilvie Loft, and Bernard Ominayak,[1] who have brought their concerns to Ottawa only to find themselves ignored or silenced. Why we now know about them, why their stories are recorded in the history books at all, is that they went to inordinate measures for their causes.

Kashechewan too was overlooked; at least, until something extreme happened there. The E. coli crisis put it on the map in October of 2005. It was one of those stories that built slowly, but then was everywhere — in the national media, the international press. Even then Prime Minister Paul Martin was involved.

It might not have generated all the attention had it not been for another water debacle that had happened five years earlier: the Walkerton crisis. Seven people had died and twenty-five hundred had become ill because they had drunk water contaminated with E. coli, even as those responsible, utilities manager Stan Koebel and water foreman Frank Koebel, denied there was anything wrong and told the public that the water was safe to drink. Both would eventually plead guilty to a charge of common nuisance through a plea bargain. Many felt the sentences — one year in jail for Stan and nine months of house arrest for Frank — were a little lenient, especially as they admitted to falsifying reports and Frank admitted to drinking on the job and having a beer fridge at the facility.

That incident drew attention to the water crisis in First Nations communities. Here we were in a country with 60 percent of the world's lakes, with one-fifth of the world's fresh water, and still there were an estimated seventy-five thousand[2] people without fresh drinking water. We were, and still are, a country that has a special Disaster Assistance Response Team (DART) that can fly anywhere in the world and produce clean H_2O out of the world's filthiest sludge. But these capabilities have not translated to action: what's a crisis elsewhere is normalized within our own borders, and DART specializes in foreign deployments rather than fixing the same issue at home.

Kashechewan's water crisis, coming on the heels of the previous one in Walkerton, highlighted the difference between how water safety is handled on- and off-reserve. In the rest of Ontario, the Walkerton crisis spurred the passage of the Safe Drinking Water Act, which demanded better training, plant operator licensing, frequent checks of the system, and fines for those who did not comply. But for First Nations communities, water is not a provincial responsibility, but a federal one, and the provincial legislation was not implemented, nor were comparable federal regulations and systems.

Beyond water, the crisis gave the community a reputation. Around the world, it became symbolic of a larger problem. The American media spoke of its Third World conditions, saying that its infrastructure was poorly built and "continued to worsen." The shoddy buildings, failing water, and unpaved roads had come about because we as a nation had failed to uphold "basic human rights,"[3] according to the *Associated Press*, dated November 13, 2005. Other equally damning indictments followed. According to Austrian newspaper *Die Press*, it was representative of the "terrible situation [on Canadian reserves] and the failure of the [Canadian] government to raise the living standards of its Aboriginal peoples."[4] No longer just an issue of bad water, Kashechewan became totemic of the government's failure to address the problems faced by First Nation's reserves across the country.

Kashechewan's population is a mere 1,800 people; that, combined with its remote location and lack of supports, ensured its citizens were ill-prepared to deal with the attention. A third-grade teacher, a graduate of Nipissing University's Teacher's College in North Bay, who was originally from Guelph, had gone there and found it difficult to cope with her four-month stint in the town. She wrote about her experience for the *National Post* in an article titled "All the lost boys and girls," dated November 19, 2005. It wasn't just one incident — and these things rarely are — but the event that most disturbed happened in her own classroom. While at the white board, some students began to throw dead rats and mice at her. Afterwards, the students did not settle down as the teacher pleaded, and instead chopped off her hair. The teacher later wrote that she had been unable to move on, and from the tone of the article, she still harboured resentment.

The crises continued, as did the media coverage. Take the prison fire in January 2006 where two men died. They died because the jail was badly run: it lacked fire extinguishers, smoke alarms, and sprinklers. Guards heard Ricardo Wesley, twenty-two, and Jamie Goodwin, twenty, shouting "Emergency! Emergency!" as the foam mattress on the floor of their cell became engulfed in smoke and flames. Meanwhile, prison guards fumbled with unlabelled keys.

Afterwards, there was an inquest to examine just what had gone wrong. First, there was the issue of the fire department. There wasn't one. Kashechewan didn't have any firefighters, fire trucks, or hoses. With every electrical fault or errant lit cigarette everything could be lost in a night of flames. And the jail was falling apart. That was the conclusion of the 2009 inquest. That wasn't news to the band council, who had written to Ottawa several times complaining that its jail was beyond repair. Outside experts had agreed. Five years before the fire, there had been a report prepared by the Real Property Consulting Group for Public Works and Government Services Canada, which found that the conditions of the Kashechewan detachment were "very poor," and recommended the jail be "demolished and rebuilt."[5]

The inquest had examined the morale and capabilities of the staff. They were demoralized. Some police officers "needed to be mentored,"[6] according to Wesley Luloff, from Long Lake First Nation at Longlac, and a twenty-three-year veteran with the RCMP, who had left to become a staff sergeant with Nishnawbe-Aski Police (NAPs) in 1994. They had no one to train them. At the time of the blaze, Kash's NAPs was staffed entirely by local officers. It had been like that since 1994, part of the national push towards Native sovereignty, a historic movement that had been slowly gaining ground since the Red Power movement in the '60s. It had been an important victory for generations of Native activists, a way of solidifying the relationship between locals and police.

Nearly everyone agreed with the ideology behind the move. But finding people with the right qualifications had been challenging. Most people in Kashechewan — 70 percent — leave school before grade twelve and there were not enough high school graduates to staff the precinct. No matter, they had gone ahead with the local hires anyway. They would learn on the job.

After the fire, the decision was upended. People had died. It must not happen again. There was a decision to raise the police to the same standards as everywhere else. That meant the same educational qualifications. And so, in a move that reversed the 1994 decision, the Kash force began to recruit outsiders with more qualifications to manage the station, and other remote communities, such as Fort Albany and Attawapiskat, followed suit.

Chief Solomon did not mention the reversal when he spoke to the inquest. Instead, he asked the jurors to see the bigger picture, claiming that the news stories failed to capture the challenging reality of Kash life. He was pleased they had made the trip to the reserve and taken the time to come to town and talk to the victim's families. They got a taste of life up north, he explained. But he warned, presciently, it was only a glimpse. The day trip wasn't enough to discover its harsher aspects. It is one thing to drop in, talk to a few locals and leave, he said, "but to actually live it is a different story."

The crises continued. In January 2007, there was the attempted suicide pact. Twenty-one people decided to kill themselves — mostly minors, including a nine-year-old. The coverage of the story itself was strange: what surprised was as much what was missing in the reporting as what was published. The reporter did not mention why the kids wanted to kill themselves, who else may have abetted them, the kids' method, or their parents' reaction. Instead, we were told vague things: on February 7, 2007, the *Toronto Star* quoted the Deputy Chief Philip Goodwin, saying, "I don't really know what's going on." That same week, in the *Globe and Mail*, the health director Edward Sutherland was quoted as saying, "we fear something terrible is going to happen."

After that story, I scanned the newspapers waiting for more details, but none came. Once again, the reserve had emerged from obscurity to full-blown crisis and back again within just a couple of weeks. Such upsetting issues don't just disappear. Determined to find my own answers, I headed up north.

ONE

Moving North

The interview did not last long. Ten minutes, fifteen tops. A meeting on July 28, 2010, with Kashechewan's Chief Jonathan Solomon at Toronto's Delta Chelsea hotel to decide whether or not I can live in his community for five months. That I am sitting here trying to move north to a community known for its bad water, fires, and youth suicide problem is strange to both friends and family, curious to myself even, although I understand that, in my obsession, I need, if not answers, then a little clarity. So I sit among brown leather couches and glass coffee tables and wait.

A building consultant from Georgina Island named Kevin Whitlock has arranged this meeting. He's an acquaintance of an architect friend of mine from Toronto who for some reason seems to have taken a liking to me. Which is excellent as he's both tight with the community's chief and has an insider's knowledge about Kash, having been there many times since 2005, consulting with its leadership on their housing and infrastructure. Over the phone, he's told me a few things about Chief Solomon. He's in town for governmental meetings and has a reputation for being progressive, levelheaded, and politically savvy. I think he said these things to put me at ease, but I'm still nervous and I wipe my sweaty palms repeatedly on my rumpled grey suit.

Surveying the guests in the lobby, I wonder which of them might be a First Nations chief. A man of medium build, about five-foot-nine, catches my eye. He's not what I am expecting. He wears a black baseball cap, ironed dress shirt, pressed blue jeans, and has steady blue eyes. We exchange glances, and he walks towards me, then sits down.

"So you're the reporter."

"Yes, I'm Alex Shimo."

"Nice to meet you. I'm Chief Solomon."

We shake hands.

"So I hear from Kevin Whitlock that you want to come to Kashechewan? Why?"

I pause. "Well, it's been in the media a lot. I'm sure there's a lot more to it than the media makes out."

"Yes." He nods slowly and holds my gaze.

"You've done a lot of work fixing the community. Like with the water plant." I had heard this through Kevin.

"Yes. The water is fine now."

"It would be good to have a story that covered this."

"It would." He pauses. "And you can sell *this* story?"

I nod, hoping I actually could.

After that meeting, I sit by my computer and wait. That I am able to meet with Mr. Solomon to discuss my trip is a modern luxury. Had I been scheduling a visit thirty-one years ago, I would have had to do more than just talk to the chief, I would have had to obtain written permission from Aboriginal Affairs and Northern Development Canada (AANDC), or since it changes its name so often, what Aboriginals sometimes call the Ministry.[1] That's because under the old Indian Act's so-called "Trespass laws," you could be arrested by the RCMP for arriving on a reserve uninvited. Anyone visiting a reserve needed permission from the government. The law was meant to discourage Natives from moving between reserves as a way to control the population — and for the most part it did. In many such communities, there are jokes about the fact that everyone is related, and has the same surname. The Trespass law was modified in 1985,[2] and today, Aboriginals are allowed to move between communities, but only if they get the permission of the chief. Outsiders, too, need permission to visit a reserve. That's the law according to the Indian Act.

A week before arriving in September, I am given the go-ahead. With the news, I begin calling around, following leads on people who might put me up. Connecting is a struggle — there isn't a cell phone service and few have voicemail. When I finally get through to someone, the phones often cut out, and the line is dead when I redial. Another issue is the lack of space. There are no hotels, motels, or bed and breakfasts. Nor any spare rooms. Residents are jammed in tightly in Kashechewan — 1,800 people crammed into 274 one- to three-bed bungalows — which means that people sleep in garden sheds, on floors, or anywhere there's a spare nook. I haven't found accommodations by the time I leave for Kash.

I spend my drive north shouting into my cellphone, begging for someone to take me in. By the time we arrived in Timmins, I have a lead. A third-grade teacher, Emma Foray, might be able to help. She doesn't have a spare bedroom, but she does have a doorless broom closet, and if she can find a curtain and a mattress, I'll be allowed to stay.

My driver is Kevin Whitlock. He's a history buff whose conversation moves effortlessly and thoughtfully between seemingly disparate topics. He has the insider's take on nearly every story, perhaps because he's a leader in his Ojibwa community or because he has worked with many of the First Nations communities in the news. What he really wants, he says, and the reason why he's going out of his way to help me, is for someone to tell the tale of the community in a way that's more than capital letters and screaming headlines. How, he asks, are we supposed to move forward with any real understanding when only the most extreme crises are covered?

In Timmins we stay overnight in a cheap motel, and the next morning we visit a Chinese restaurant where they serve chicken balls for breakfast. Kevin says he needs to pick up some food because there aren't any restaurants in Kash and, he adds, the best way to sweeten the mood and break the ice is to deliver takeout food. Apparently, the chief's assistant has already called ahead with Kevin and put in her order.

We grab the paper bags, get back in the car, and drive to Timmins airport. Then we board a Piper plane. We've been joined by four construction consultants who work with Kevin, making us six altogether. The Chinese food at our feet, we take off.

Shouting above the roar of the engine quickly tires our voices, and one by one, we turn from the group to look outside. We're squished together in the tiny plane, an aluminum speck above the forested boreal expanse of the Canadian Shield. The winters are harsh in this subarctic climate: the average temperature is minus two degrees Celsius, and the average winter temperature is minus sixteen degrees Celsius. As I was soon to discover, it's damned cold and biting too: the James Bay area is also one of the windiest places in all of Ontario. Yet the fall is majestic. We fly below the clouds and their shifting lilac shadows animate the landscape below. The tiny black spruce trees glow deep green in the sun or darken underneath the roaming cumulus. Flecking the emerald is all manner of colours: tamarind horsetails, maroon tamaracks, pink orchids, and northern bluebells. A herd of caribou bolts from the timber and gallops through a sunlit glade. Wild grass runs up to the Albany River and a few families fish in canoes and motorboats on water that gleams blue and yellow in the afternoon light.

The turbulence focuses our attention back to the plane. It's shaking so much that I wonder about the liquids inside my luggage. Like many reserves, Kash is supposed to be "dry." I'd been told the law before I left Toronto. Which I promptly ignored. I like a drink to take the edge off things and to quiet my busy mind. Once I knew the rules, I made it my business to discover how to circumvent them. It wasn't hard: I poured a couple of bottles of vodka into a few Gatorade bottles, then dyed it blue. After we land, I wait for the security officials to board the plane and check my bags. I have never smuggled anything before and I suddenly panic. What was I thinking? What if they unscrew the lids on the Gatorade bottles and smell what's inside? What if all my clothes have been dyed ultramarine? My need to drink might cost me my trip and a couple of months' work, I realize. But luckily, perhaps because I'm with Kevin, our luggage is not searched.

We walk across the dusty gravel to the airport — a few windswept orange cones and an aluminum shack — and wait for our ride. Inside are some PVC moulded chairs and a security guard dressed in a fluorescent-orange vest playing endless rounds of solitaire. The airport is too small to comfortably hold the six of us, so we wait outside by the chain-link fence. Twenty minutes later, a middle-aged man arrives in a dark-blue Ford van. The consultants, who are here for a day trip to examine home heating and ventilation systems, decide it's most polite for the "lady" of the group to sit in the truck cab. Our driver, Sinclair Wesley, tries to wipe off some of the dirt that blankets the truck's interior. On route, he jovially points out the truck's war wounds — the back door is missing a handle, and the wipers are operated by a wire bent through the window. The windshield is an intricate gossamer of cracks.

We drive into town, and as we approach the reserve's main street I get my first glimpse of Kashechewan. It's already been in the media a lot, and I've spent many an hour gazing over newspaper photos, but I am still hypnotized by its alien landscape. I look out over the one-story, pre-fab buildings, dirt lots, criss-crossed lines of laundry, and it reminds me of a refugee camp. Everything looks like it's built so it can be quickly disassembled, as if it wouldn't matter if it was occupied, or if all the residents suddenly disappeared.

Next to the road is a graveyard where some of the white plywood headstones have been knocked down, and mounds of earth and overgrown scrub replace flowers. Its chain-link fence has been flattened. Children play with the dirt by the side of the road. A girl of about seven sits in a ditch, playing sandcastles with a split bag of concrete.

The wooden houses are covered with warnings about "bulletts," "gunz," and "fuckin," the faded graffiti half usurped by more recent additions. On the roofs, children play on the overhanging satellites. In the yards are rusted vans, some burned out and others with swastikas drawn into the dust along the side.

Next to the dirt road four boys, none older than twelve, stand in front of the corrugated aluminum building that houses the community skating rink. A boy in a black hoodie stands ahead of the group and gazes at the rink's light. Holding a rock in his clenched fist, he fixes his eyes on the target. The town is quiet and I can hear the boy grunt with the rock's release. A miss, then the two-toned *clunk-ping* of rock hitting metal. The boy turns and silently joins his friends. No one makes eye contact; another steps forward clutching a stone.

Ignoring the boys, we drive to the office of my future landlord. If I am to live with Emma, I need the permission of her landlord, Rosy Sutherland. As education director for the Hishkoonikun Education Authority (HEA), she has multiple roles: she is responsible for Kashechewan's two local schools and landlord for the teachers' housing, including my rented broom closet. Hishkoonikun is one of those dark jokes that Crees tend to make about their own troubled situation: it means "that which is left over," i.e., the reserve land that no one else wants.

Sinclair Wesley and the others drive off, saying that they will return in forty-five minutes after my interview with Ms. Sutherland. I sit outside her office and wait. Ten minutes later, she opens the door. She wears a pressed blouse and rectangular glasses. She has soft brown eyes and delicate features. I had read about her mother, Minnie, in a book about police injustice and racism called *Fireworks and Folly: How We Killed Minnie Sutherland*. Like other stories about Kash and its residents, hers was widely covered in the news media and scored itself onto the national consciousness. The ignominy was in its avoidability: her death could probably have been prevented if the authorities had done their jobs. On New Year's Eve 1989, Minnie, who had moved from Kash to Ottawa and was legally blind, was knocked down by a car on her way to see the Parliament Hill fireworks. Finding booze on her breath, the police dragged her by her coat from the middle of the road to a snowbank, then left. When an ambulance was finally called, they took her to a detoxification centre rather than a hospital. In reports, police called her drunk and a "squaw." Lack of appropriate medical attention led to her death from a blood clot in the brain ten days later. The book and newspaper reports suggested that racism contributed to her death.

Ms. Sutherland doesn't say anything about this history, and keeps the interview brief. She seems tired. I figure she doesn't want to talk about it, and with her approval, I wait outside her office for Sinclair. We drive to my new home. Emma, the teacher who has agreed to put me up, lives at a group of houses at the centre of town called "the teacherage." All the buildings in Kash had been renumbered a few months earlier, but none of the old lettering taken down, so some have multiple numbers, others just broken bits of font. The numbers are confusing, so I stash my bags in someone's yard and go door-to-door asking where she lives. Her place doesn't have a doorbell, so I call out her name.

"So, how was your trip?" she asks, coming to the door and picking up two of my bags. She has a kind-looking face and a short, mousy brown bob.

"Long!"

She shows me around her one-bedroom apartment. It's clean and spare. The largest room in the house is her kitchen, where there's a stove, fridge, a couple of wooden cupboards, and a tiny kitchen table that doubles as her desk. Towards the back of the room are a brown '70s-style couch and a

TV, which together comprise the entirety of the living room. The pièce de résistance is a bread-maker that she's brought up from her home in Toronto.

"Cozy!" I say, trying not to trip on the peeling kitchen floor tiles.

We walk to my broom closet. It's big enough to fit a mattress but nothing else. That's okay; I don't have anything else to put in the room except clothes. Since there aren't any drawers, we decide to create space by removing the books from the shelf above the bed.

"I'm sorry," she says. "Everyone is very packed here. This *is* Kash."

We walk into the living room. Emma doubles as the town librarian. Without a working library, her house is filled with books, which are stacked on shelves, behind the sofa, and in piles on the floor. Children ask for them day and night. She teaches me a special knock to use if I forget my keys — one used by all the teachers — to distinguish us from them.

After I've finished unpacking, I go outside for my first look around. I walk south towards the river. It is calming in its immensity; at 982 kilometres, this is the longest river in Ontario, draining through James Bay into the Hudson Bay watershed, the largest of its kind in Canada. Four continental glaciers advanced and retreated over the region during the past million years grinding down the granite and gneiss of the Canadian Shield, and salt and fresh water flowed in, saturating the land. Everything is wet — the muskeg soil, the peaty moss, the spongy lichen, the swamp smartweed, the water lilies — all dripping into the myriad small lakes, bogs, and seemingly interconnected streams that feed into this great river. For thousands of years, these waters have been the engine of life, local grocery store for fishers, and business hub: the Albany was the main trading route for the Cree people, and even today, there is a brisk trade between neighbouring communities once it freezes to become the winter road.

I leave the river and descend the dyke to the reserve. The sun is fading behind thickening cloud. Looking up, I realize there are no birds. The missing wildlife is heightened by another absence: the lack of green. Kashechewan has no flowers, grass, or trees. Everything looks hard and beige. And when the wind dies, the air feels thick. As if the weight of expectation hangs in the air.

Next to the houses are teepees, but they don't look anything like the taut bison skins I have read about. Traditionally, teepees were conical leather tents, decorated with fox pelts and other skins. Today, they are made of tarp or black garbage bags and draped in sodden, greying blankets. When I peak inside, I see they are full of strange things: half-eaten bloody birds — still feathered — dirty dishes, cigarette butts, and dolls.

It doesn't feel like a place for children, and yet they seem to be everywhere. They play in bunkers of soil underneath the houses, in ditches, on top of roofs, hanging from TV satellites. Kashechewan's birth rate is 37 per 1,000 each year, 340 percent higher than the rest of Canada. (The figures are similar for other James Bay reserves.) I look across the street and see a boy and girl playing house by a rusted, tire-less van. The doors are open and the girl, about six, crawls inside. Clambering over the seats, she kneels on a car seat strewn with shattered glass. Thankfully she's wearing jeans.

The boy, about seven, climbs on top of the hood.

"Look at me!" he shouts, standing and jumping up.

She leans out the cracked window, her smile framed by perilous shards of glass. I turn away and three young girls, who look between six and nine, run to me and look up expectantly, asking for candy. When I shake my head no, they ask for money or cigarettes.

I head back to Emma's, thinking about all I have seen. I have told the chief that I want to live here for five months. It's a long time, but previous stories about First Nations for CBC radio and *Maclean's* magazine have always taken much longer than anticipated. But I now wonder whether I'll be able to cope with an extended stay. I worry that the ever-present decay will seep into my bones and tip me over the edge.

I've hardly walked a few steps when I hear what sounds like an engine purring. I turn around. Pointed teeth and grey fur. A stray husky.

Traditionally, dogs held pride of place for First Nation communities. Survival in the bush depended on healthy, well-trained canines. There was an emotional bond too: they were brothers in spirit. It had been like this for as long as anyone could remember, perhaps longer: their connection was explained in the Cree-Ojibwa creation myths. It began with the very first man named Anishinabe, the primordial human, who formed a friendship with a wolf. Together they roamed the planet, learning about the plants and animals and discovering why they were put on this earth and what it means to live a good life. These dogs don't seem to be my spiritual brothers.

The husky is joined by another, and they approach, teeth bared, growling.

"Git!" I shout.

They don't. They continue to inch toward me.

"Git!" They are a few metres away now. I frantically scan the ground. I find a rock and throw it. It lands softly, with barely a sound.

"Go! Git! Go!" I stamp my feet. They pause, then resume their approach. I turn and bolt.

It is just a few metres to the nearest house.

"Please!" I shout, near crying. "Please let me in!" I hammer on the door. It opens.

"Huh?" says a man of about forty.

"The dogs," I say, and point to them.

He steps outside.

"*Awas!*" he shouts. "*Awas!*"

"Can I come in?"

Fifteen minutes later I leave his house holding a two-by-four. At home, Emma is busy marking school papers. I've been afraid of big dogs since the age of seven, the lingering anxiety triggered by memories of being regularly knocked over and pinned to the ground as a small child by a Doberman pinscher who used to roam the neighbourhood. The word on the street was that he was aggressive with small children because his owner was violent and beat him. Perhaps it was true or not. It was one of those inner-city London, England, neighbourhoods where people kept to themselves unless something was seriously wrong.

I am upset but Emma seems deeply involved in her work, so I don't tell her about what happened. Instead, I try to call my girlfriend Jill who lives with her two-year-old son in Santa Fe. I really want to talk to someone, but can't get through.

Over the next few days, I sleep a lot and attempt to work. I am trying to finish a magazine article on two Russian translators — Richard Pevear and Larissa Volokhonsky — who are supposed to have revolutionized how we think about the books like *Anna Karenina* and *War and Peace*. I started it before I left but didn't have time to finish. No matter, I thought. I'm headed somewhere isolated and it will be peaceful and quiet. How wrong I was. The issue is the noise. Everywhere on the reserve is loud. There are the sounds of ATVs, garbage trucks, cars and vans, teenagers playing soccer outside, kids playing tag in the road. There is no more traffic, than say, downtown Halifax, but we are living on a bog in a place where the walls, floors, and ceilings are paper-thin. Each time an ATV passes the furniture rattles.

At first, I decide to simply work outside. I climb up on top of the dyke, and find a spot on the hill that looks out onto the river. But no matter where I go on the reserve, the issue is the stray dogs. They seem to have a special fondness for my bottom. After being chased a few more times, I stop working outside, and instead, I email a friend in Toronto to send me some earplugs so I can work indoors. And I decide to go to the doctor's. The dogs are stirring up long-forgotten memories and panic, and I need sleeping pills.

I have suffered insomnia on and off since university. If I'm under a lot of pressure, I find it hard to turn off my busy mind. The not-sleeping causes anxiety, and my mind races against itself. It's been a while since I was stressed enough to have a serious bout, but once it takes hold, the sleeplessness can last for days, sometimes weeks.

The nursing station, a grey bungalow building, is a few blocks away. A sign on the door says, "No more condoms, sorry." The floor is littered with flattened cardboard boxes — doormats to lessen the grey dust. Everyone is in stockinged feet to help keep things clean. I take off my shoes and wait.

Dr. York[3] is the town's main doctor. He only flies in once a month, so I am lucky that he's here. We introduce ourselves, and then I ask for a prescription of sleeping pills.

"Already?" he asks.

"Yeah. I sometimes get insomnia."

"How long you here for?"

"Five months."

"Five months?! What will you do?"

"I'm not sure yet."

"Well, why did you come?"

"I was going to do a story on the water plant. How it was fixed. The chief thought it would be a good idea."

"The chief? That's funny given the history."

"What history?"

"Never mind. I probably shouldn't tell you."

"Tell me what?"

"Well, we live in one of the richest countries in the world and turn a blind eye to what's in our own backyard."

"I don't understand."

"Don't you see? No one cares because it's Natives. They've heard it all before. So they needed something different. Something that would make international news. Like the 2005 water crisis."

"Yeah I read about that."

"I was sitting right here," he says, pointing to the armchair next to the window. "I was watching about twenty reporters outside my window. They had all flown in from across Canada to cover the story. But it was all made up."

TWO

The Fourth World

Chess and Checkers sat in the kitchen of Thomas's house and chewed on wish sandwiches. Two slices of bread with only wishes in between.
— Spokane/Coeur d'Alene author and poet Sherman Alexie

I take a taxi back from the nursing station, mulling over what Dr. York has told me. The water crisis put Kashechewan on the map. It made the reserve famous. That the leadership would have a sufficiently intimate understanding of the media to know how to get themselves noticed, and to deliver these fabrications without anyone suspecting anything, was, if true, pretty astonishing.

At home, I walk inside, open my computer and begin looking at various sources online, trying to figure out the veracity of what Dr. York has told me. On the web, there are different versions of the E. coli story. In the online *Canadian Encyclopedia*, it says there is "confusion swirling around the Kashechewan crisis," and questions were "raised about whether Kashechewan's delegation to Toronto had played up the water issue to get the attention of politicians who otherwise ignored them." On the CBC website, it has no such mention of any uncertainty or any exaggerations regarding the water issue. The E. coli crisis, it explains, was legitimate; after the initial bacteria scare, water plant engineers put too much chlorine in the water until it was at "shock levels." This worsened residents existing skin conditions, including scabies and impetigo, and forced the evacuation of the town.

I chat with a producer friend of mine, Aaron Brindle at the national CBC radio show *The Current*. I explain why I'm living in Kashechewan First Nation reserve and the conversation I had with the doctor. I tell him everything I've heard and I ask him whether he thinks it would make a good radio documentary for his show.

He's intrigued. He encourages me to follow up on the lead, and that if it turns into something, I'll need to explore the why of the hoax and give a good indication of people's motivations, not just how it happened. People will have to go on the record and I'll need to tape them with studio-quality recording equipment in a quiet place to have good sound.

Quiet place, I think. How will I do that? Everywhere is noisy. At best the sound lessens after 9:00 p.m. Maybe I can convince people to stay up late, and schedule any interviews for those times.

I go to the fridge to snack while I think. There's no food left from what I brought with me, so I take a taxi to the Northern Store to buy groceries. We drive to another house to collect a family of four on their way to a birthday party. In the car, we make small talk about our favourite types of cake. In the Cree spirit of egality, all the taxis operate like buses: the car picks up as many passengers as possible, with everyone paying four dollars regardless of the destination.

Hungry, I decide to stop at one of the local stores a few metres away to grab a chocolate bar and coffee. Most of the stores sell Tim Hortons with Coffee Mate. I stand by the counter, and sip.

A red triangle of light glides across the room. Through the store's window, duct-taped together, I see the police. The car stops and then idles behind a young twentysomething man wearing a hoodie; an officer gets out and roughly pushes him into the cab. Silently, he gets in without a fuss. They drive off.

"What was that?" I ask the clerk, a middle-aged man named John, after describing what has happened.

"Justice Day," he says.

"What are they doing?"

"Gathering everyone up for trials."

"Where?"

"Where there's space. At the skating rink."

With more questioning, he explains. The judge flew in this morning from Cochrane. Since he's here just for the day, the police only have a few hours to round up all the perpetrators and witnesses listed in the case. Most trials don't take very long, as people tend to plead guilty, because they don't commit crimes unless they are inebriated, and so, given that the reserve is supposed to be dry, the plaintiff assumes they must have done whatever is being suggested as they've already done something wrong. For this reason, the Cree expression for police, *ohgoo-baysow* means "someone who locks you up." The mistrust of the system has become part of the language.

It's a familiar story. Aboriginal people are more likely to plead guilty to crimes they have not committed, according to several studies. They are also more likely to be racially profiled, according to other reports.[1] They are less likely to be given bail and they serve longer times for the same crime than someone who is non-Native. The presumption of guilt exists before the crime. If the studies are to be believed, and there have been many of them, this idea exists in the mind of the Aboriginal person, and on the other side, in the judges, police, and all involved in the criminal justice system. Consider the case of Maisy Marie Odjick, who disappeared in 2008 and whose mother, Laurie Odjick, has been active in pressing the public for a national inquiry into murdered and missing women and girls. In Odjick's case, the police investigating — the Kitigan Zibi Anishinabeg Nation in Quebec — did not seem overly concerned when Maisy went missing, and assumed that she was living a "risky lifestyle," according to Laurie. As a result, the investigation into her disappearance did not begin until a formal search was conducted three months later. Sometimes, what happens is even more troubling: the victims are physically intimidated, as contended by New York-based group Human Rights Watch. Interviewing fifty Native women and girls in ten communities between Prince George to Prince Rupert, B.C., on the relationship between indigenous women and the police, they documented several incidences of women who had been strip-searched, tasered, and raped, which were discussed in their February 2013 report. Occasionally, what transpires is worse than rape. They are dragged to the snowbanks to die, as happened with Minnie Sutherland.[2]

Elimination of police brutality was one reason for the creation of NAPs — so that Aboriginals would not be treated on reserves as occurs in the rest of Canada. I stare out the window looking for clues as to whether it has worked. The police car passes again but does not stop. I wait for it to return but it does not. I walk to the Northern.

In the entrance, the shop clerk, a Cree man in his twenties wearing oversized sweats, frisks all the Native people entering the shop. There has been a recent bout of shoplifting, he explains. Lining up, they wordlessly raise their hands, while he pats them down. He lets the white customers through without questions.

Once through, I walk up and down the aisles. Leaning on their shopping carts, people walk as if in a long dark tunnel. No one makes eye contact. No one raises their voice. Hunched, they slowly shuffle beside shelves filled with food they can't afford under flickering fluorescent lights.

The Northern Store is unlike any I've visited. It sells everything that one needs for life up north: cans of tuna fish are crossways from ATVs, heads of lettuce near canoes. When the stores first opened in the late seventeenth century, these goods were purchased with furs. In 2009, the shop stopped accepting them, according to trapper Bobby Wynne, forty-six, and today most send their furs by mail to places like North American Fur Auctions, then spend the money at the Northern. It's more of a hassle, but it means that they get a better price, he says. It's a complaint more than two hundred years old: as a result of the bans on First Nations trade, they have long had monopoly power, explains Edmund Metatawabin, a Cree author and activist. The furs were underpriced, he says, and most fell into debt.

I walk past thirty-dollar frozen pizzas and fifteen-dollar cartons of eggs. At the fruit and veggie section, a bunch of grapes (seventy-nine grams or about one hundred grapes) costs $13.42, a bag of apples (three pounds of golden delicious) is $15.29, and a single head of red cabbage is $12.89. The prices don't reflect the quality: the veggies are dry or browning, and some of the meat is past its sell-by date. I choose only the cheapest items: a bunch of green onions on sale for $2.69 and some apples.

Then, I walk to the tinned goods section, where a crowd lingers. There's a special on Klik canned meat: today it's only $5.99 for the smallest tin.

"What's Klik like?" I ask a twentysomething man named John, wearing jeans, runners, and a bandana patterned with tiny Canadian flags. He's the first person to make eye contact.

"Salty," he replies. We both laugh.

"The prices are crazy here," I say.

"Yeah. Not like down south."

I pick up a can of tuna fish. It's $5.29. "I don't understand it. How do you survive? How does anyone survive?"

"You gotta eat tha' Kash diet."

"Huh?"

"Klik, eggs, and tomato soup," he replies.

"Is that healthy?" I ask.

He shrugs. "It's what we can afford."

He returns to his shopping cart full of tins.

I walk to the pasta section. Mac and cheese is on sale; it's only $2.50 per box, a steal, and only a dollar more than down south. I stock up. Next to me a twentysomething woman in a plaid shirt sidles up to me, examining the brands of mac and cheese. Two young kids jostle for position in her cart.

"Settle down," she whispers. She pauses and scratches her arm. Visible beneath her shirt cuff is a rash of raised red circles that look, to my inexperienced eye, like ringworm. I want to ask her about it, but she turns away, and covers up.

I finish my shopping and walk to the shopping clerk. I was careful in my selections; I have abstained from buying any fresh meat, fish, or fruit. Mostly I've bought mac and cheese, pasta, and tuna fish. These were the staples of my childhood, when my mother, recently divorced and a struggling artist, did her best to make the pennies last. My two luxuries were green beans and chili oil.

I stand at the checkout and nervously watch the numbers spiral upwards. My first grocery bill comes to $342.57. I take out a wad of fifties.

Fuck, I think. How do people survive on the $383 monthly welfare? I work full-time and I still don't have the money to live.

I take a taxi home to avoid being chased by the stray dogs. Once home, Emma and I make dinner together and discuss the prices at the Northern Store. It's a big problem, she says; some of her kids come to school without breakfast or supper the previous night. She knows when it happens because the kids tune out or misbehave. Sometimes, she says, they eat paper, likely to quell the hunger pains.

We finish our meal, and then sit down to watch television. There's a knock at the door. I answer it. A middle-aged woman and her daughter of about six stand on the doorstep. "You like Cree art?" asks the mother.

I nod. The woman opens her plastic sack and holds it up. Birds are stacked on top of each other. I take one out and hold it to the light. Twigs curve at sharp angles, like a delicate exoskeleton. It smells like a spruce forest.

"I made them myself. They're geese. Ten dollars each. Or thirty-five dollars for a family."

I return to the living room and get my wallet. Returning, I buy two geese.

"Any more?" she asks. She gestures to her daughter. The child picks out a bird, and holds it up for me to see. Her wide eyes look like tiny saucers. Her mouth is smudged with something dark, and her hair is matted. She reaches forward, offering it, like it's a gift.

I know that I should keep buying. I can see that this family is desperate. Twenty dollars is hardly anything. Just about enough for a bag of oranges at the Northern Store. Not enough for a whole pizza. Certainly not enough for a full meal. That's what my conscience says. But I suddenly feel panicked. I shut the door.

I have always brought back suitcases full of stuff whenever I've been in developing nations, like Cuba or Tanzania. Kash is like those places in some respects, such as the shared taxis and people selling homemade goods door to door. But not in terms of cost. Although its population is desperately poor, with 86 percent of its population surviving on welfare, the prices are some of the most expensive in the world.

In terms of income, on average, its population earns an estimated $9,741[3] per person, which includes the salaries of those who work, and the 86 percent of people who survive on welfare alone. This is slightly below Statistics Canada's on-reserve average of fourteen thousand dollars. If it were a country, Kashechewan's income would be ranked at 104th in the world, below Iran (70th), Namibia (101st), and Sri Lanka (103rd).[4] But these statistics do not give a true indication of its poverty. In Iran, Namibia, and Sri Lanka, the salaries are low, but so too are the prices. The cost of fresh produce is usually less than in Canada. In Kashechewan, the wages are low, but the costs are four times as high as in the rest of the country.

By including purchasing power parity, the relative incomes in Kashechewan fall even further. They are more aligned with South Sudan, Haiti, and Afghanistan, all economies that have been ravaged by conflict and war. For this reason, indigenous communities in Canada and North America are sometimes called the "The Fourth World," rather than the Third.

Life in the Fourth World means that in a country that is one of the world's leading net exporters of food, people often go hungry. According to a 2014 Council of Canadian Academies study,[5] 90 percent of the Dene Nation of the NWT said that they or other adults in their household ate less or skipped meals as they couldn't afford to eat regularly. This is true for other First Nations communities in the North, according to the 2007–08 International Polar Year Health Study, which found that Canada had higher incidences of food insecurity than other developed countries with indigenous populations, such as United States and Greenland.[6] "The emerging public health crisis in northern Canada represents serious concerns that require immediate attention," the Canadian Academies study espoused. In the short term, it recommended more food banks.

Things are not supposed to be this way, at least not according to our own laws. We have signed national legislation and international treaties outlining our commitment to adequate food, including the 1948 Universal Declaration of Human Rights, the 1966 International Covenant on Economic, Social and Cultural Rights, the 1989 Convention of the Rights of the Child, and the 1998 Canada's Action Plan for Food Security. These laws and treaties look at what is required for a person to thrive and function in society. They have argued that safe, nutritious, and sufficient food is part of society's contract with its citizens. Access to food taps into the very pillars of Canadian society — justice, community, health — and for this reason is as much social justice concern as basic human right.

When explaining why practice and policy are misaligned, why we have ignored those national and international commitments and promises, a familiar story surfaces to explain how things came to be, and it's a narrative that is used in many of the studies. Less land meant that the Crees could not continue to rely on hunting and trapping, which had been how they supported themselves for thousands of years. Small catch sizes led to fewer skins, a phenomenon that was compounded by falling prices, as fur coats fell from fashion and people turned to cheaper materials. That created less incentive to trap, which meant lower incomes and higher food expenses. The Kashechewan Crees could not afford to feed themselves.

Land is key, but so too is another issue, one that unfortunately is often left out of the histories and case studies. Which is what happens behind the scenes, as the local leadership attempts numerous methods to solve their own food issues. Sometimes, the request for lower-priced food takes the form of policies that will improve access to cheaper food, such as petitions by several of fly-in First Nations in Manitoba — Webequie, Nibinamik, Neskantaga, and Eabametoong — to the Ministry for the funds to build an all-weather road. Food prices fall with better transport as people buy in bulk from down south, and then sell these goods in the mom-and-pop stores. Others, such as Onion Lake Cree Nation in the 1990s, have tried to bring in outside investors to build farms.

When Kashechewan's leadership took over from the Indian Agents in 1985, they examined the history to figure out how to solve their food issue. The common perception of northern life is that farming is impossible because of the climate. The James Bay area is in the subarctic region of the Canadian Shield. The growing season is only 140 days long. Frosts can occur on any day of the month. Acidic muskeg soil sits atop impermeable granite rock. Not the most ideal of conditions, however, there are small, secluded spots with better drainage and grass, well-suited to small family operations. Besides, Kashechewan's leadership already knew what was possible because they had witnessed it first-hand. In the nearby residential school St. Anne's, there was a successful farm and greenhouse ensuring fresh food for the staff year-round.

The leadership thought that it could be replicated. So in 1990, they started with chickens. The plan was to organically raise twenty-five broilers and twenty-five egg-layers in a wooden barn, which they planned to heat during the wintertime with a wooden stove. The leadership put together a seventeen-thousand-dollar proposal with profit margins and growth rates, and they sent it to the Ministry. Three months later, they received the response: "Does not meet feasibility requirements." It was the first of many such refusals.

What's puzzling to many is that the reserve's leadership believed they were operating within the Ministry's desired mandate. That Aboriginals would become farmers had been an Indian and Northern Affairs Canada (INAC) priority since the introduction of residential schools in the late nineteenth century. First Nations were sent to the institutions to learn how to till the land, so that they could abandon their hunter-gatherer lifestyle to establish small-scale farms across the country.

The gap between official Ministerial agenda and what happens on the ground — between promises and reality — is turning into a theme of reserve life. I have only been here a little over a week, and I have seen it manifest on the issue of food, farming, and economic prosperity in the local stores. If Dr. York is right, and the 2005 E. coli crisis is not what has been reported, then the reserve is not the only party with something to hide. I don't have any concrete proof yet; it's just a hunch, one that would be an intriguing theme for any radio documentary, but requires confirmation from someone in charge. I decide to set up a meeting with Chief Solomon.

THREE

Meeting the Chief

I'm here in plain, dusty, boring old Wasaychigan Hill ... Wasy ... waiting ... waiting ... nailing shining shingles with my trusty silver hammer on the roof of Pelajia Rosella Patchnose's little two-bed-room welfare house.

— Cree playwright Tomson Highway

Had this been a straightforward feature story, like the hundreds I have covered for the CBC and written for various newspapers and magazines, I would have simply arranged a meeting with the chief. That I didn't was partly due to rumour, but mostly circumstance. I came to write a story about the water plant. What I had heard from Kevin and others was the chief was proud of all that he'd accomplished. Since being elected in 2006, he had achieved what eludes many cash-strapped leaders of northern reserves and installed the essential manpower and systems to ensure 24-7 drinkable water. Mr. Solomon had upgraded the filtration system, introducing a new computer system, chemical mixing room, and river pumps. Unfortunately, none of the locals had passed all the licensing tests,[1] so the plant was now managed by a guy named John Gentile, who was also a regional manager with Northern Waterworks, a firm based in Red Lake, Ontario. He and his team flew to the reserve for two weeks, then left for two. Not the cheapest of solutions, but it was considered necessary so that they didn't become burned out by the Third World conditions on the reserve.

That's the story the chief seemed interested in having covered when I met him at the Delta Chelsea hotel. And given that our conversation had been extremely short, I could only presume that was what he had told the band council to convince them that my stay would be a good idea.

If I visited him now and said, "so I'm not actually writing about fixing the plant, but instead am investigating rumours about how your reserve staged a water crisis," I worried about the consequences. If it had been me who had been misled, I would be angry. And even if they were more generous than I would have been in their situation, the reserve had a quick, no-nonsense approach to dealing with those who broke its rules. They were banished in what was called, in the slang of Kashechewan, being "BCRed." It stood for Band Council Resolution. The band council met and issued a decree that your presence was harming the community. You were given a few hours to leave town.

Like many aspects of the reserve, the genesis of the BCR was shaped by its history. Until 1985, the First Nation leadership didn't have much control about who could come and go on a reserve. Only the Ministry, or their representatives, the Indian Agents, decided who was welcome to visit or live in the town. And only they chose who must be removed from the community, whether it was for breaking the laws of the Indian Act, or simply disagreeing with their decisions.[2]

From the First Nation's perspective, it was never the right people who were banished. Medicine men such as Fort Albany's John Metatawabin were locked up in the 1920s for practising their Cree religion, while those suspected of manslaughter,[3] such as St. Anne's gym teacher, Brother Lauzon, were allowed to operate for years with immunity. Complaints about these people went nowhere, according to author Edmund Metatawabin, who thirty years later organized the former student meetings that led to the court cases against the perpetrators. (Mr. Lauzon was never tried for his alleged crimes as by the time of the trials in the mid-90s he had already died of cancer.) No one wants that situation to reoccur or to feel powerless again. Hence, the introduction of the BCR rule to remove people who are seen as hurtful to the reserve.

Rather than interview Jonathan Solomon, I decide to meet other members of Kashechewan's band council. The first to agree is James Wesley, its executive director. I've already been told a few things about him. He's said to be a Cree renaissance man: hunter, father, former NAPs officer, Kashechewan leader, and a remote consultant and manager for the Quebec-based Cree Construction Development Company. A clean-shaven man in his fifties, Wesley greets me in his office at the band council. At first we make small talk, or the Kashechewan version of it, which as usual, is pretty weighty. He says that Kashechewan has a birth rate of sixty per year (higher than Haiti), and that given the Ministry's funding, it is difficult for the band council to maintain the current levels of services.

I ask him what happened in October 2005 with Kashechewan's water. His story is pretty straightforward. There was an E. coli outbreak in late 2005. Afterwards, there was a warning by the band council not to drink the water. The two schools were closed and the local radio station issued updates on the situation daily. By October 26, the water was still unsafe to drink, so the reserve was evacuated. At this point, I probably should have mentioned Dr. York's version of events. But my mind darted back to stories I had heard about being BCRed, which were upsetting, so I merely thanked him for his time.

At home, I again research online anyone who might be involved. I find another clue. A *Canadian Press* newspaper article dated October 19, 2005, states that Kashechewan's contaminated water was causing "gastro-intestinal disorders, headaches and fevers." Deaths from the issue, says that article, "are more difficult to prove." Then it quotes Deputy Chief Rebecca Friday: "It's not tolerable. It's not acceptable."

This is good. It implies that the band council either thought contaminated water was causing gastrointestinal disorders, headaches, and fevers, or they told the media that's what they believed had happened. I've already heard a few things about Friday. She is said to be extremely passionate about First Nations rights and ambitious: she is currently taking online courses to complete her bachelor's in social work from Ryerson. I put out a few calls to her and then I wait.

In the meantime, I decide to approach the chief at a local Thanksgiving feast that's happening next week. Perhaps the festive atmosphere will loosen people's tongues. The feast has been top of mind for the past few days. In a place where some go hungry, and most survive on canned meat and tomato soup, these will be abundant free food, including fresh meat recently caught by the reserve's hunters. Among locals, the phrase "wild meat" elicits a reaction like an oenophile speaking about his latest undiscovered winery, which of course leaves me asking questions about what it's like — purportedly nothing like the bland, packaged meat we are used to down south, but otherwise indescribable.

On Thanksgiving at lunchtime, a crowd of several hundred descends on Francine J. Wesley High School. We queue to enter the building, then once in the gym, line up for our food. About 250 people are in front of me. A few chat softly, but most are silent. Filling the hallway are children who laugh, eat, shout out, play tag, with a few playing soccer with the floor's garbage.

While waiting, eight men wearing baseball hats and bandanas walk to the centre carrying a moose-hide drum. A steady beat vibrates through the floors, accompanied by haunting throat songs, like the high-pitched lament of a warrior.

People leave their food, and approach, taking out their phones and video cameras. As does the chief, wearing a giant white and brown feather headdress, who smiles and nods his head in time.

The community feast, chief's headdress, and the performance by the town's band Chakapesh (a Cree mythological hero) at the town-wide feast are said to be three ways that the chief and council are bringing back the Cree traditions which were banned until 1951 under the Potlatch laws. Afterwards, they were officially legalized, although strongly discouraged by the priests and staff at the local residential schools, who taught that any indigenous cultural activity was devil worship. Since the last residential school did not close until 1996, the effects of that discrimination are still highly visible. For example, in 2005, when third grade teacher Laurie Gough tried to encourage her students to try traditional drumming from instruments that they had made, a group of Native elders told her to stop because they didn't want "evil Indian ways against Jesus."[4] And when, a couple of years later, Cree elder Paul Wesley, fifty, decided to instruct the children of all ages in those Cree traditions he had learned from elders in Alberta (because few in Ontario knew them after the century-old legacy of the residential schools), he was told by school staff to cease because the parents had complained, believing it was morally wrong.

After the performance, I'm at the top of the line. I pile my plate high with goose, moose, duck, bread rolls, and potato salad. It's such a relief after the mac and cheese and cans of tuna fish that I've subsisted on since arriving because of the Northern Store's prices.

Locals were right. The meat is nothing like what we eat down south. The flesh tastes like a well-worn muscle, metallic and musky, but underneath are the flavours of everything the animal has eaten: moss, grass, and bark. It is like eating Stilton, having lived one's whole life believing that Kraft Singles comprised the full diversity of cheese.

And now is my moment. I approach the chief, but am told by a local man, presumably one of his handlers, to wait until after he gives his speech. For twenty minutes he speaks in English and Cree about the importance of family and the strength of community. A few clap. Again, I step forward. But I'm too slow. Locals inundate him with questions and then he's out of time.

The following day I visit him at the band office, a ramshackle blue bungalow decorated with pink hearts, which I later find out is a not entirely successful attempt by a local teacher to cover the curses underneath. Inside a twentysomething man mops continuously, trying to remove the perennial dust from the unpaved roads. I pass him and a sign that said "*shawaylimick keshayhowuk*," and the English translation: Respect Your Elders. Another gives a number of a lawyer to call for victims of the Sixties Scoop. A Toronto-based law firm, Wilson Christen LLP Barristers, is gathering names from First Nations communities across Ontario for a class action lawsuit.[5]

The Sixties Scoop is the historic phenomenon where the provincial child welfare services removed children from their reserves for adoption, usually to non-Native families in Canada or the United States. In Kash, one to two children were taken per year from 1960 to 1989, according to Andrew Reuben, former chief of Kashechewan, who lived through it. (The Ministry did not keep these figures.) Nationally, an estimated twenty thousand Métis, First Nations, and Inuit children were taken from their homes during the same period. In theory, the practice was supposed to target only those children who had been either neglected or abused. In reality, Ottawa assumed that the child, by virtue of living on a reserve and growing up with parents who had been in a residential school, must be from a broken home. Government representatives — usually someone from the Ministry — would fly to the reserve and announce that the children were required for "medical tests" or "a doctor's appointment." They were rounded up from around town and would leave by airplane. The parents would wait for them to come back, then as it slowly dawned on them that they had been lied to, they would ask questions. "We were told that our children had been taken far away, but that we shouldn't worry, because they were in a better place," Reuben says. "We knew that we were being lied to but we had no one to complain to because it was the authorities themselves who were stealing our children."

Staring at the sign, I think about the word *scoop*. To me, it sounds like something one does unthinkingly to an inanimate object such as ice cream; and like many terms invented to euphemize history, it sanitizes the story, which resembles state-sponsored kidnapping.

Once again, Chief Solomon is busy. There's not enough room to wait by his door so two of us stand, and the others take the chairs around the corner. Through the door, I can hear the chief consoling a woman who is pregnant with her sixth child. She lives with her parents and two sisters and their children: sixteen to a house. The living situation is standard for Kashechewan; most homes are overcrowded with extended families living under a single roof.

I don't mean to eavesdrop on her conversation. I never wish to snoop, not on my downstairs neighbour Ken Reid, the computer teacher, who after work, calls to tell his wife how much he misses her, nor on Emma speaking to her twentysomething daughters about which Kashechewan children come to school hungry. But all the walls are paper-thin: like so many things in Kashechewan, they are custom-built for the reserves. I hear them and they me. No one has any privacy. This is not an environmentally specific adaptation, because what the reserve actually needs in places of extreme temperatures and regular flooding is houses that don't fall apart. Instead, they are given flimsy walls that gain holes with the slightest touch. The adaptation is for the same reason that most things disintegrate on the reserves: to save on costs.

The chief speaks in a deep and calming voice, telling the woman that he'll support whatever she decides, baby or abortion. The couple emerges from the chief's office, and woman continues to weep softly. As I approach the door, a fortysomething man taps me on the shoulder. It's an emergency, he says. He'll only take a few minutes.

Through the door, the man tells the chief that he hasn't received his OW (Ontario Works unemployment benefit). Mr. Solomon explains he'll look into it. The people keep coming: the man who can't pay his six-hundred-dollar heating bill, a thirtysomething woman living with her seven children in a house where all the windows are broken.

On the reserve, the chief is responsible for all of these issues. Mr. Solomon and the band council do pretty much everything. They are landlords of the reserve's houses, responsible for plumbing, electricity, and repairs. They are the main employers in town, hiring people to work at the band office, water plant, and for the winter roads. They act as workplace supervisors and human resources managers. They act as family counsellors and therapists. They are responsible for garbage collection, snow removal, road repair, and street lighting. They deal with things such as fixing the broken windows and graffiti removal. They manage the municipality's responsibilities, such as fire protection and extreme weather. They deal with the province's jurisdiction too, such as healthcare, education, and economic development. And they are legally responsible for anything that might go wrong on a reserve, such as flooding or arson.

At first glance, the First Nations government seems to have too much power. But there's also a strange shadow side to the legislation, which limits responsibility: every time the chief does anything, any time he wants to spend money, he must clear it with the Ministry. Under sections 35[6] and 53.1 of the Indian Act, reserves are Crown land. All resources on a reserve belong to the state. There may be a public language of Native sovereignty, a nod to political correctness, but the reality is the Ministry manages most reserves, at least indirectly, as they see fit.

It is technically possible to opt out of these laws, to gain a modicum of sovereignty under the First Nations Fiscal Management Act, but in order to be eligible, the First Nation must first prove that they have stable finances, which for reserves like Kashechewan is basically impossible, because without industry or natural resources, the community is almost entirely dependent on Ottawa's funding.

Kashechewan is unable to opt out, a reality that it shares with 475 — 75 percent — of Canadian reserves. It is tied to the grim realities of the

Indian Act. Governance becomes an obscure and mysterious procedure that resembles, at least to an outsider, a bureaucratic version of Oliver Twist. To get anything done, Chief Solomon must file an application with the Ministry — a development grant or contribution agreement — and wait.

The problem with this process is that Mr. Solomon has also almost zero information on how the department makes its decisions. He's not alone; none of the chiefs interviewed — Andrew Reuben (Chief of Kashechewan 1993–95), Edmund Metatawabin (Chief of Fort Albany 1986–96), Leo Friday (Chief of Kashechewan 2000–06), Chief Shining Turtle of Whitefish River First Nation of the Anishinabe (Chief 2003–present) — knew the process for awarding funding, why some projects are considered worthy and others are not. It is difficult to fathom why Fort Albany has been given flooding protection but Kashechewan has not. Or why Fort Albany has drinkable water, but Neskantaga First Nation and another 75,000 people do not. Or why some reserves — Six Nations of the Grand River in southwestern Ontario, for example — have a fire department, while many that have been in the news after children have died in fires, such as St. Theresa Point First Nation and God's Lake Narrows, both in Manitoba, lack this basic service.[7] The reserves are forced to play the lottery where the prizes are the basics of survival, such as drinking water or affordable food.

These issues are not Kashechewan's alone. They are the reality of most reserves, as documented in the 1996 Royal Commission Report on Aboriginal Peoples (RCAP), which highlighted some of the ways that, because of their financial structure, the reserves were unable to function, to use their powers to achieve fair, effective, and accountable government. It detailed the inevitable frustration and delays caused by this system of governance. And the report went further, arguing that grasping the limitations on First Nations governance meant accepting the stasis built into the system, and that necessitated understanding the numerous ways that the reserves have been deliberately impoverished.

According to the report, from the nineteenth century onwards, First Nations were confined to poverty in six ways. They were moved away from mineral wealth. They were displaced from natural resources including forests, lakes, and rivers. They had their land stolen through "theft" and "fraud" (RCAP). They were stopped from establishing their own industries on traditional land. They were obstructed from opening other businesses. They were excluded from jobs off-reserve through racism.

If you take away a community's ability to generate resources, and then remove an individual's ability to make money, then according to the RCAP, you end up with the current situation of First Nations: racialized poverty. The statistics bear this out. Ninety-two of Canada's one hundred poorest communities are Aboriginal, according to Statistics Canada. Half of First Nations children live in poverty. In Canada, the median income is fourteen thousand dollars[8] for First Nations people living on-reserve, compared to thirty-three thousand dollars for everyone else, or less than half.

"The historical record has much to say about the current impoverishment of most Aboriginal economies," explained the RCAP. "It is also instructive about the factors that must be addressed if development is to proceed according to Aboriginal priorities."

To overcome the toxic legacy, urged RCAP, Canada cannot simply continue along the status quo. The system will not magically right itself. Addressing a historic mistake will take positive and sustained action, it urged. There must be a serious redistribution of rights, land, and resources, and an active stand against racism. Otherwise First Nation governance of Kashechewan and other reserves without an economic base will remain "an exercise in illusion and futility."

Standing outside his door, I wonder whether Mr. Solomon ever thinks his job is an exercise in illusion and futility. From his impassioned speech at the Thanksgiving feast and how he is helping those in his office, it doesn't seem like it. I am at the front of the line now, and thinking of what to say, when the thirtysomething male receptionist approaches to say that he's very sorry but the chief is required for a band council meeting. Can I return tomorrow?

And so the waiting continues. The following day, I am told that he has gone to Timmins for meetings. This process, whereby people stand outside his door, does not start with him, but with the Ministry. It has a reputation like that of a satellite Soviet state: wait times of years are common and applications sometimes get lost. The quickest way to circumvent the bureaucracy is to have an in-person meeting with a Ministry representative, which is where Mr. Solomon is said to be.

Reserves that want to break free of poverty must file an application with the department. Consider Onion Lake Cree Nation, Saskatchewan, twenty minutes north of Lloydminster. Like the people of Kashechewan, the Onion Lake Plains Cree pride themselves on autonomy and self-reliance. But by the early 1990s, this former hunting community had gone through the same economic changes as the people of Kash. Eighty percent were on welfare. Fortunately, things were looking up: the First Nation had secured an investment partner to build a potato farm. Now they needed building permission from the Ministry. So the reserve wrote and waited. And waited some more. Eventually, the investor got bored of waiting and took his business elsewhere.

Or there's the Beardy's and Okemasis First Nation, Saskatchewan, located near Duck Lake. They share a history with the Onion Lake First Nation: they are also Plains Cree who once lived according to the migration of the buffalo. After the animals were hunted almost to extinction, incomes and employment fell. But by 2012, this community had diversified, and managed to lower its unemployment rate to 30 percent. The turnaround was instigated through a partnership with the federal government in the opening of the Willow Creek Healing Lodge, one of the first prisons based on Aboriginal principals, where elders from the community visit prisoners, and emphasize spiritual growth and rehabilitation. To further stimulate economic growth, the leadership approached the Mennonite Farming Association to train young people in a farming program. The Mennonites were excited, but at the time of writing the program still has not received Ministry approval.

Or the Okanagan Indian Band. It's one of the eight reserves forming the Okanagan Nation Alliance, whose traditional territory spans the Canada–US border, in Washington State and B.C. The reserve emphasizes economic growth through sustainable industry, and is located in a particularly lush and beautiful part of British Columbia, known for its wineries, water sports, and sockeye salmon. In 2007, Joyce Beattie and his business partner James Louie, decided to set up some properties on their Okanagan reserve. This time, unlike the Okemasis or Onion Lake Cree Nation, the Ministry responded. It said that the practice was illegal as the designated rent — one dollar — was too low, and the only way that the businesses would be permitted was for Mr. Louie to hire a lawyer and surveyor to obtain the correct rental price. Mr. Louie refused as he already had a business arrangement with Mr. Beattie, and both had agreed on the price. The correspondence went back and forth over the months, but as time was running out to secure his investors, Mr. Beattie and Mr. Louie took the matter to the Canadian Human Rights Tribunal, who said that the current laws treated First Nations "like children." In response, it gave the Ministry a warning,[9] telling them to be careful about how they interpret the current laws. The legislation remains unchanged. The waiting game continues to trap First Nations in poverty.

This situation isn't only pointless, explains Leo Friday, former chief of Kashechewan, it's also a Catch-22. For the reserve to escape poverty, they need capital. Without private investment, any funds must come from the Ministry. But it won't lend the reserve any money because, without any employment, they won't have any income to pay it back. Which means they don't have the money to create employment schemes and they can't leave poverty: "INAC always tells us that we need 'a financial recovery plan,' for them to loan us any money," explains Reuben. "But we can't develop such plans because we need jobs to generate money."

The first plans for Native-run employment schemes began in the mid-80s. Until that time, the band council and chiefs wanted to develop them, but their hands were tied. Kashechewan was run by Indian Agents who flew into the reserve and dictated all policies and legislation themselves. Technically, reserves could run themselves, but only if they could escape another Catch-22: they had to prove they were sufficiently technologically advanced to manage the social programs created by the Ministry. Since all Natives were required by law to go to the residential schools (where the dropout rates were about 80 percent) that meant most people who might, in theory, be able to take over the running of the reserves could barely read or write. Without good schools, the Ministry often decided, without testing or interviewing the population, that the leadership were not sufficiently competent to manage their own affairs, and instead, the Indian Agents flew to the reserves every four months to tell them what to do.

This was standard operating practice until 1985. By then, the civil rights revolution had spread across North America had given rise to the first Canadian Aboriginal organizations, such as the National Indian

Brotherhood, the Union of British Columbia Indian Chiefs, and the Federation of Saskatchewan Indian Nations. Those organizations and the newly created Assembly of First Nations were demanding better living conditions on the reserves. The growing pressure and awareness led to the major changes to the Indian Act in 1985. Reserves like Kashechewan were now responsible for their own economic development.

With the changes, the leadership met and began brainstorming about ways to end the poverty. After two months, they came up with a plan to create the first Native-led employment program to tackle the then 90 percent unemployment rate: an environmentally friendly fishery in the area. The Albany River is prized for its fresh, clean water, and strong currents, which create perfect conditions for many northern species including walleye, pike, and trout. The band council gathered information about the environment, fish handling, breeding, growth rates, and profit margins. They compiled a proposal and budget and sent it to INAC. The pilot project would cost an estimated six thousand dollars. We don't know the reason why Ottawa thought it was a bad idea, since the reserve sent them a detailed operating plan and budget, but never heard back, and today, they have no record of such an application. Three months later, they resubmitted the material. Same thing. No response.

Without the official explanation to understand why they had been turned down, the band council came up with possible explanations, explained Reuben. Perhaps something about their proposal did not accord with the many pages of laws and procedure that must be satisfied for any development proposal to be approved by INAC. Perhaps the Ministry did not want a fishery. Or maybe, it was the sums of money involved or that the fishery would contravene the anti-trade sections of the Indian Act, which banned Aboriginals from doing business with each other unless the transaction was approved by the Ministry, laws that were only revoked in December 2014.[10]

The local leadership didn't have any answers, but in 1986, they tried again. They would build salt evaporation ponds on the southern James Bay coast. They would start small, with a few metal collection pans and washing the salt in a bathtub at a nearby house. If successful, they'd expand. The pilot would cost two thousand dollars.

The Ministry didn't reply. So they wrote again. This time they were given a reason for the rejection. Ottawa said that any salt produced should be tested by Health and Safety for it to be saleable, and they did not have the resources to set this up. Unfazed, the following year, in 1987, another scheme. An ask for five thousand dollars to start a tree nursery. Ottawa said no. There weren't sufficient funds in the budget for employment creation. And so it has continued over the years, the reserve creating ever more ingenious employment schemes, and the Ministry finding ever more creative ways to say no. There has been the fifteen-thousand-dollar clay-mining project in 1991, the ten-thousand-dollar pig farm in 1993, the fifty-thousand-dollar lumber yard in 1993, the twenty-thousand-dollar greenhouse in 1995, and the twenty-thousand-dollar dairy farm in 2000. "You name it, we've thought of it," explains Reuben. "We've basically tried everything over the past thirty years. We send them budgets. We send them proposals. It's always the same."

Five weeks after I first tried to interview Mr. Solomon, we sit down together. Thirty-five days may seem like a long wait for an interview, but is relatively short in Kashechewan terms. It's nothing like the time that Roxanne Hughie had been waiting for a new house (fifteen years). Nor does it compare to the time that Arthur White has been trying to obtain a construction job (two years). But I do not have the patience of my Cree friends, and am fed up and frustrated.

Chief Solomon makes small talk — what did I think of the Thanksgiving feast? I tell him it was moving and he smiles. He questions whether I am enjoying Kash. I lie and say yes. And then, because I am nervous, I do not question him on the rumoured hoax, instead I ask what he knows about the 2005 E. coli water crisis. He says that I should contact then Chief Leo Friday, who is now Grand Chief of the Mushkegowuk Council in Moose Factory. It's back to the drawing board again.

FOUR

A Lead at the Garbage Dump

The best way to kill a man is to pay him to do nothing.
— Québécois singer Felix Leclerc

By the start of November, I was desperate. I had $5,050 of debt, a few tamarack birds, a rumour about a water scandal, but little else. That would probably have been a good indication that I should pack up and go home, especially with the growing frustration and unease that I had felt since arriving. But, unfortunately, life is not lived with the benefit of hindsight. Besides, I did not want to have to admit to Jill, my friends, and my family that I had invested all this time and money and had failed. I worried that the CBC would come to believe that I was the type of person who promised more than they could deliver. So I went looking for work.

Job hunting in a place with 86 percent unemployment probably wouldn't have occurred to me, except for the story of Chris Mead. A forty-one-year-old who ran the school's food and nutrition program, he decided to use his down time to get to know the community, by working a couple of shifts at a local store run by Bobby Wynne. After a few months, he was let go, partly because they had run out of work and also because he had been trying to sell the customers healthier options, like juice instead of pop, although no one could afford it.

Working for Bobby, Chris had picked up a few words of Cree, and some understanding of the local culture. The effect he had on the community was apparent. Everyone spoke highly of him. They said he was fair, and that despite the colour of his skin, he didn't look down on anyone.

Arriving at Bobby's, I feel immediately at home. The size of a large living room, it's not only one of the largest stores in town (other than the Northern), but it has the greatest variety of goods, selling not only the usual pop, coffee, and potato chips, but canned meat, chili, and household supplies.

When I ask how he has managed, he says it took him twenty-seven years to open it. His dad taught him to trap, and he started working at age seventeen taking tourists into the bush. After a couple of years, he found extra work in construction and elder care, and he saved every penny until he had $120,000, enough to buy lumber to build the store by hand.

Unfortunately, there is no work right now, but he recommends that I check back in three months time, as he will start to sell takeout food — hamburgers, chicken, and fries — and he may be in need of a cook.

The next store is Philip Goodwin's, again a wooden bungalow that's slightly smaller than Bobby's, which sells coffee, chips, chocolate, and in the back, fried food. He says that there aren't any vacancies, and again recommends that I check back in a few months.

It's the same with Henry's.

That any business exists in Kashechewan is a small miracle. Technically, all trade is banned on the reserve, under section 92 of the Indian Act.[1] Other laws make running a business very difficult. Business vendors and investors are not allowed onto the reserves without first obtaining Ottawa's permission. Any decision to be made about the land — how it can be used, what sort of businesses can open, the terms of investment — must first be cleared with the Ministry. "The Indian Act ties our hands," according to Ron Abraira, director of the Kahnawake Economic Development Group, speaking to the Royal Commission on Aboriginal Peoples. "It says you can have all the businesses you want as long as they're no bigger than a French fry stand. This perpetuates the underground economy."[2]

These bizarre rules are a product of the nineteenth-century attitudes that shaped them. Back then the federal Ministry considered wealth a corrupting influence on Aboriginals. There was something good and honest about "their wild state," according to the general beliefs of the time. That innocence was debased when they made contact with money or modernity. They became damaged goods. The "noble savage" disappeared, and what replaced him, according to Canadian parliamentary discussions, was either a "drunkard" or a "debaucher."[3] To "save" them from the vice that paved the road to influence and power, First Nations needed to be controlled.

To get around these laws, most Native-run stores are hidden in plain sight. Without signs, storefronts, or awnings, they look like every other house on the block. On the balance sheet, they are invisible too: everyone operates strictly in cash.

The poverty above ground is in stark contrast to the riches below. Some of the nation's biggest deposits of precious stones and minerals have come from the area around Kash, as it has very old craton rock, ideal for mineralization. Most cratons are deep underground, which make them harder to access, but those in the James Bay area have been pushed to the surface due to extreme temperatures and weather erosion. The biggest pink diamond in Canada was mined in 2012 near here at De Beers's Victor Diamond Mine. The value of diamonds in this area are said to be the second highest per carat in the world.

Before arriving in Kashechewan, I had expected that some of these riches would be reflected in the reserve's economics. That's what is supposed to happen according to many academics and the media. Mining will "lift First Nations out of poverty,"[4] according to the *Globe and Mail*. It is "the only form of economic development that could reduce the impoverished, third-world living conditions in First Nation communities," according to the magazine *Canadian Mining*.[5]

Creating good jobs and wealth for the community is what many believed would happen when Kash signed the 2009 Impact Benefit Agreement with De Beers. It is easy to understand how this idea might have come about. The company does not release its revenue figures, but assuming that the mine is operating at its full capacity of 600,000 carats per year at diamond grade, and given today's prices of $520 ($400 US) per carat, revenues should be approximately $3.8 billion annually ($2.9 billion US).

Several locals interviewed said it was hard for impoverished First Nations to negotiate Impact Benefit Agreements (IBAs) with a company like De Beers because they could not afford to retain expensive lawyers, given that the band council was co-managed (i.e., too far in debt to run their own affairs) and their population has Fourth World poverty.

Kashechewan has received some money from De Beers — nineteen million dollars — although currently that money hasn't been touched, as the community wants a safety net to deal with its ongoing crises, explains Oliver Wesley, current director of the education authority. What they really wanted was jobs: "That was the initial agreement with De Beers and us. It was in the memorandum of understanding. Employment would be developed. There was supposed to be royalties and revenue sharing. It didn't happen."

Actually, the section of the IBA focusing on employment is more tenuous. What is promised is more guiding principal than hard employment numbers. There will be "opportunities to maximize business participation by promoting and encouraging the use or development of qualified [First Nation] businesses whenever possible and practicable in supplying services." And that Aboriginals will be given priority to any "project-related activity within the First Nation Homeland," but only if the persons "demonstrate the competence and qualifications."[6]

The wording matters because of the modernization of the profession. Men in hard hats shovelling coal for a canary's wages no longer dominate today's industry. Instead, it's become specialized and high-tech. Every position listed on several mining employment sites requires at least a high school diploma, from the white-collar jobs, such as chief financial officers and environmental managers, to those who operate the machinery, including blasters, crush operators, and electricians. Even the security guards need at least grade twelve. Forget getting your foot in the door fresh out of school, according to journalist and career expert Philippe Dozolme. "The young guy starting as helper to experienced miners and learning skills on the job tends to be an image of the past," he writes in an article entitled "Top ten things you should know before searching for a mining job." "The increasing complexity of the mining process and involved technology nowadays requires a much higher level of skills, including computer literacy."

This would be great if First Nations like Kashechewan had a great education system so they could demonstrate that they had sufficient "competence and qualifications." But they don't.

As a result, almost everyone living near the mine — including reserves Kashechewan, Fort Albany, Marten Falls, Moose Cree, Weenusk, Attawapiskat — is First Nation. Most people working for the mine are not. A couple people from Kashechewan sometimes work at the mine, says Julie Wesley, who used to work for the De Beers Victor Diamond Mine as a housekeeper, tidying the staff's on-site residences. However, these people generally aren't employed directly for De Beers, she says, but instead for Attawapiskat Catering LP which provides the mine with menial services — cleaners, janitors, and cooks.

For a couple of measly minimum wage jobs, the cooking and cleaning positions on the band council job board generate a lot of excitement. Most of the time, locals rarely raise their voices, and I never hear gut-jiggling laugher. But outside the job board, there's positive buzz. People approach and smile at the new postings, and unlike in the grocery store, they make eye contact. Some say "hi" — or the Cree equivalent, "*wachay!*" — and I want to feel happy for them, to share in the job excitement, but I can't help wondering how many hundreds of people from the other reserves near the mine are competing for the work.

Curious as to whether the mining situation should be part of any possible radio documentary about Kashechewan, I stand at the job board asking questions. After interview requests to half a dozen people, Arthur White is the first to say yes.

"We can talk, but not here," he whispers. "Someone might hear."

"Okay," I reply. "Where to go?"

He points to the door.

Once out of the building, he explains his reasoning. He's heard I am asking more questions than I should — questions unrelated to the fixing of the water plant, which is supposed to be the reason that I'm here. By broadening my research, I am undermining the original agreement. I'm breaking the rules, he says, and it's making everyone nervous.

I sympathize. I had hoped to write about the water plant, but "First Nation chief fixes filtration system" is not a story that will easily sell newspapers. And after arriving here, and hearing people's stories and seeing the conditions, I believe that there's a lot more that needs to be said.

"Yeah," he says. "We're trapped."

"How?"

He shakes his head. He doesn't want to speak in the open.

We walk away from the band council while discussing places to meet. Arthur is willing to talk, but only if we find somewhere private. Easier said than done. The reserve lacks amenities and public space. There is nowhere to meet: no parks, coffee shop, restaurants, or an out-of-the-way bar. We can't go back to my place as my broom closet room doesn't have a door. Arthur is one of the few people on the reserve who lives alone; however, he is still nervous about going there as he believes that neighbours will talk.

We arrange to meet at the garbage dump at the edge of town a few hours later. As a meeting place, it has several advantages. This being mid-November, some of the food waste is already partially frozen, so it doesn't smell much. Located five hundred metres from the reserve, and surrounded by trees, it is out of earshot of the normal buzz of ATVs, trucks, and cars that roar through town. And, although people occasionally come to scavenge on weekends, on weekdays, like today, the place is deserted.

We arrive separately ninety minutes later. Thankfully, no one is there. The place has a faded beauty, with furniture precariously stacked on top of cars. Most space is filled not with food, but by barely used metal things — cars, trucks, fridges, stoves, bikes — discarded not because they can't be used, but because there are no tools to fix them.

As we talk and walk, Arthur, thirty-three, tells me his life story. It's similar to many on the reserve. He's a hunter: geese are his specialty. In his grandparent's day, in the 1950s, that would have been sufficient to get by. But today, the prices and catches aren't what they were, and like most, he survives on the $383 unemployment benefit. Sometimes, he manages to find part-time work filling gas, construction, or cleaning garbage. That's about it. Lots of his friends have already given up, he says. They sit on their couches, watch TV, and try to find enough money to eat until they are next given their monthly cheque.

He believes his situation is not sustainable. Without a salary, he cannot afford to eat healthily. Instead he survives on mac and cheese, canned meat, and the occasional wild bird, when what he would really like is some fresh fruits and vegetables. If he could eat better, he would have the energy to go to the bush more.

He can't stay in Kash, nor can he leave. For the past two years he's been unemployed. Nor does he have much education: he dropped out of high school to care for his dying grandparents. If he leaves the reserve, he worries he will end up on the streets. He has heard stories of people in Kash going south for work and finding nothing, returning penniless, or ending up homeless.

"You could help," I say.

"How?" he asks.

"By bringing awareness of what happens on the reserve. Telling the real story."

"You think it will make a difference?"

"Yes," I say.

We sit on a rusty car. I began to question him in-depth. He tells me he's heard that the water crisis wasn't what it seemed. But his knowledge is limited: he doesn't know who in Kashechewan's leadership was involved or how it might have been organized. Fortunately, he knows of one revealing detail: river water was used as a prop. This was because the water coming out of the taps was clean in late October 2005, or thereabouts (he wasn't certain about dates), but still needed to look dirty to convince the incoming officials the crisis was ongoing. I need more information, including who collected it, and he says he will ask around and get back to me.

I ask him if he thinks that the 2005 water crisis ended up helping the community. A bit, he says. Before it happened, the people of Kashech-ewan were desperate, even more than today. They had tried to improve their situation through grow-food initiatives and employment programs. They had been promised help. But each time, those words came to nothing. If I want to understand why the leadership might have done it, he says, I should examine why the relationship between Kashechewan and the Ministry has broken down.

That failed dynamic hasn't always been the case. Several times throughout history, Kashechewan was poised to reverse its fortunes. But it never happened, which could be, I have begun to believe, the reason why they would turn to something as desperate as staging a water crisis. And with Arthur's information, exactly that is looking increasingly likely.

It began, in 1978, with oil. It had been five years since the first oil price shock, and energy costs were crippling all of Canada except Alberta. The Mackenzie Valley Pipeline was supposed to solve some of these issues by feeding northern Alberta with natural gas, but it had been effectively killed the previous year with Justice Thomas Berger's inquiry. The unstable global conditions led Ottawa to look further afield for oil production. Previously the Silurian rocks (444 million years ago) on the northern tip of the reserve were thought to be too young to have been subjected to enough heat to begin the process of converting organic matter into burnable hydrocarbons. But after the '73 oil shock, Ottawa began looking in obscure places, including the Silurian rocks in northern Manitoba and Ontario. Five years later those efforts were rewarded. An oil shale that started in the Hudson Bay and extended southwards into Kashechewan's land was discovered. That summer, the Ministry flew to the reserve to let them know that it wanted to develop the resource.

Superficially, it sounded like the perfect solution to the reserve's problems. In 1978, the economic situation was as bad as it is today. An estimated 80 percent of people in Kashechewan were living on welfare at an estimated $120 per month for a single person. Not enough to buy food each month, let alone to have a healthy standard of living. Developing the resource could be a viable solution. People would need to be trained to work at the well. The roads would require improvement to bring in the drills. Pipes would have to be laid. Communication lines would have to be brought up to par. The investment could stimulate subsidiary businesses. Who knows, maybe the reserve could become a mini Edmonton or a (very) tiny Houston.

But then Chief Willie Wesley had some misgivings. As in other areas, the law that governs the reserves — the Indian Act — was not on his side. Section 53 states the Crown is responsible for all financial decisions on reserve or surrounding lands. Section 57[7] states that Ottawa is in charge of all mineral rights. Among indigenous activists, these are sardonically known as the "You have no control over the land any more, we do ..." clauses.

To make a decision on what was right for his community, Chief Wesley spoke with his band council. There were two things to consider. The history: What had happened over the past thirty years when mineral resources had been found on First Nations land. And second, whether there was any reason this time would be different.

The historic record told a familiar story. In 1950, the relocation of the Oujé-Bougoumou Crees[8] in northern Quebec would provide the template for the next four decades. When gold was found on their land, they were removed from their homes and relocated to a swampy point on a lake. It wasn't just that living on a marsh meant that their homes became mouldy, but that the Canadian government had not located them sufficiently far from the mining tailings ponds. Metals including chromium, cadmium, arsenic, zinc, and cyanide began to build in nearby Lake Chibougamau. Elder Albert Mianscum would later report that the majority of fish that he caught had physical deformities including red sores, missing eyes, and missing fins. (A 2005 study[9] found the metals' concentrations in the lake exceeded the allowable limit under Canadian Environmental Quality Guidelines.) The First Nation decided to move away from the pollution, choosing a dry spot two kilometres away. The Ministry said their new location was illegal. The First Nation ignored them and relocated anyway. The Ministry labelled them "squatters," and forcibly relocated them to a nearby campsite with one-room shacks with plastic sheets for roofs.

Most of the relocations that would take place over the next two decades would have the same plot points, narrative arc, and final act. Development required moving First Nations out of the way. It was the same story in 1952 when oil was found on the Alberta Lubicon Lake Crees territory. Or that same year when the Carrier Indians of Cheslatta Lake were moved to make room for Alcan's new aluminum smelting industry at Kitimat, British Columbia; or when the Tsay Keh Dene First Nation, then known as Ingenika, were shunted out of the way with the 1961 construction of the W.A.C. Bennett Dam in northern B.C.; or the Chemawawin Cree who were flooded from their homes to create space for the Grand Rapids Dam (1962); the relocations of the Métis of Ste. Madeleine, Manitoba (1935); Mi'kmaq of Nova Scotia (1942); the Gwa'Sala and 'Nakwaxda'xw, British Columbia (1964). The list goes on.

Chief Willie Wesley was determined that his would not share their fate: dispossessed, impoverished, and lacking compensation or legal recourse for the harms done. Fortunately, he had one new addition to his negotiating arsenal. The previous year had seen a groundbreaking affirmation of indigenous rights with the publication of the Berger Inquiry. Titled *Northern Frontier, Northern Homeland*, it marked a significant departure from how land had been historically developed. In researching his report, Berger did something rare and unusual: he listened to those living on the land. Interviewing elders from thirty-five communities, he discovered that, like the Crees of Kashechewan, they had not interpreted their Treaties — Numbers 8 and 11 — as great giveaways of the land. Their ancestors had understood them as peace accords, detailing the conditions under which the land and its resources were to be shared. The Berger Inquiry was an important shift in Aboriginal-Canadian relations, one that would pave the way for the development of the first modern First Nation treaties: the 1999 self-governance agreement of Nunavut and the comprehensive *Nisga'a*[10] treaty of 2000.

To guarantee that Kashechewan would not be dispossessed, Mr. Wesley asked the Ministry for some safeguards. He wanted promises of employment and some say in how the oil would be developed and the profits used. And environmental protection beyond what was guaranteed by the limited Department of the Environment Act. These requests were made in person to the visiting Ministry spokesperson. He nodded politely and returned to Ottawa. Over the next few months, Chief Wesley sent several letters. He never heard back.

With time's passing, Willie Wesley came to believe that the Ministry's non-response had spared the reserve. Berger had temporarily shifted the tone of the First Nation–Ottawa discourse, but it would shift back with the relocation of the Hatchet Lake Dene Nation, northern Saskatchewan (1985), due to uranium mining. There were environmental considerations too. The late '70s and early '80s were a time of many large scale oil spills: the *Betelgeuse*, Bantry Bay, Ireland (64,000 tonnes spilled in '79), the *Ixtoc*, Gulf of Mexico (454,000 tonnes in '79), the *Atlantic Empress*, Caribbean Sea, near Tobago (287,000 tonnes in '79), *MT Independenţa*, Bosphorus, Turkey (95,000 tonnes in '79), *Irenes Serenade*, Navarino Bay, Greece (100,000 tonnes in '80), and by 1982, the Ministry's lack of response had convinced the reserve that any development of oil, according to Reuben, would mean that "they would take everything, leave us with nothing and destroy the land."

Without oil extraction, the reserve switched gears on power production. By 1982, they had settled on the idea of wind power. The turbines would likely be eyesores, but they did not violate the Cree's Seven Sacred Teachings,[11] which demand that one respects the environment and everything contained within it. The James Bay area is perfectly suited, one of the windiest in all of Ontario — a combination of flat marshland, lots of open water, and high temperature differentials.

That summer the new chief, Dan Koosees, invited the Ministry to the community to measure the wind speed. When the Ministry's researcher arrived, Mr. Koosees requested that he go to the bay where the wind is strongest. The Department representative didn't listen. Instead, he measured the Beaufort scale next to Kashechewan's band office, which is at the centre of a bowl-shaped depression — the lowest point for 150 kilometres — and the slowest point for wind. Mr. Koosees never received the numerical results, instead he received a letter that told him what he already suspected: no wind.

Today, none of Kashechewan's natural resources have been developed. Several people have found what looks like nuggets of gold in the rivers surrounding the reserve, but no one has contacted the Ministry or private investors and invited them to test the rocks. "We don't want them to kick us off our land," Arthur explains. "This is our home."

After he's finished his story, I'm cold. Lending me his gloves, he gives me a ride on his ATV back to the reserve. As we drive, I mull over what I've been told. I am one step closer to confirming that the water crisis was partially staged. But with a more detailed picture of the history, the lines of justice have become blurred, and it is no longer clear who is hoaxing whom.

FIVE

Welfare

One Ministry to rule them all, One Ministry to find them
One Ministry to bring them all and in the darkness bind them.
— Cherokee novelist Thomas King

Under any other circumstances, I would have probably told Emma and my downstairs neighbour Ken, given them all big sloppy kisses, and run out and bought some champagne to celebrate my lead. But Kash was a dry reserve, which meant that the only place to buy alcohol was from a bootlegger, and it cost two hundred dollars for five hundred millilitres of vodka. Moreover, Arthur had confirmed the rumour that I'd heard: the reason why Chief Solomon had allowed me onto the reserve was that I would write a story on the fixing of the water plant. I wasn't sure whether Ken and Emma had heard it too, but didn't want to say anything that would force the question of its veracity. If they knew, they'd be in the same situation that I was: either continue my deceit, or admit that I had misled the chief at the Delta Chelsea hotel in Toronto, than not made any attempt to correct his misunderstanding.

Arthur's lead was a fluke, but in general, it was hard to find people to make small talk with, let alone interview at length. There is an issue of trust — they are used to bad things happening to their people. Out-siders have committed crimes, including the abuses in the residential schools, the loss of land, the arrests during the Potlatch laws, the seizure of children during the Sixties Scoop, and the lack of help despite promises to the contrary.

And I'm a journalist. Even if I report nothing but the facts, what they tell me could harm their community. That's the opinion of several chiefs, interviewed once I left the reserve, and Hugh Shewell, a regional supervisor for the Ministry between 1983 and 1988, professor in the school of social work at Carleton University, and author of *Enough to Keep Them Alive: Indian Welfare in Canada, 1873–1965*. The potential liability comes down to money. In Kashechewan, and in many reserves, all funding comes from the Ministry. In theory, this shouldn't matter at all. But as before, principle and practice diverge, at least according to those living it. It's not what is said, but what is implied and how the Ministry shuts down dialogue. No one says if you criticize us then we won't give you any funds. The same effect is achieved in a more subtle way, according to Franklin Paibomsai, Chief Shining Turtle of the Whitefish River First Nation, Ontario: "What they say is, 'that if you don't want to work with us, then we have other projects to do.'"

Those who criticize the system might have their funding dry up. Or they might be spied upon for civil disobedience. CSIS, the Canadian spy agency, and Canada's Integrated Terrorism Assessment Centre watched and prepared reports on the indigenous protest group Idle No More. Former Idle No More organizer Clayton Thomas-Muller says he has documents that prove that the RCMP has been keeping tabs on him since at least 2010. Indigenous filmmaker and activist Clifton Nicholas confirmed that trend, saying that he's been contacted by CSIS on three occasions.

Sometimes, the government tries to discredit those who criticize it. In 2007, the First Nations advocate and executive director of the First Nations Child and Family Caring Society of Canada, Cindy Blackstock, approached the Canadian Human Rights Tribunal (CHRT) to allege that there had been discrimination against First Nations children. Blackstock's claim was hardly inflammatory: she said that child welfare services serving First Nations children don't receive as much governmental funding as kids in care elsewhere in Canada, which is apparent from talking to anyone who works in the sector. The Ministry spied on her, tracked her Facebook page, and paid staff to follow her to public presentations and take notes, all to help win their case. One wonders why they bothered. It's not as if people are lining up to file complaints. Few people can afford to bring these cases to the tribunal due to the time and cost.

To find interviewees, I start to mill about wherever and whenever I see people. In general, most people don't hang about unless they are in a line. People queue to speak to the chief, they line up to collect their food at the Thanksgiving feast, they wait outside the nursing station for health appointments. They wait for their monthly unemployment benefit, windows and plumbing to be repaired, the cables that hang loose to be fixed, roads to be paved, flooding protection, and a fire department. The bureaucracy is organized through lines and figures: the Indian Status number, used to keep track of Treaty and welfare payments, and movement on or off the reserves; the student's residential school number; or the reserve's identification number.

At one point in history, the use of numbers instead of names was ideologically motivated and an administrative convenience. In the residential schools, it was part of stripping a person of their Aboriginal identity, a way of "deIndianizing" them as part of the cultural eradication that the schools implemented. Some writers, such as Edmund Metatawabin and Bev Sellars, have written about how it made them feel less than human, inferior, a non-thing.

In mid-November, I am standing and taking notes in one of these lines trying to report on my potential documentary. One hundred people are lined up in front of the Northern Store. Some smoke. A few quietly chat. Others huddle together as wet snow whips through the wind. It is 8:15 a.m. on Monday, and everyone is waiting for 9:00 a.m. when the shop opens and its manager begins handing out cheques.

Last night, this seemed like a good idea. The welfare queue was one of the few places that I knew people would have to huddle together. But I hadn't considered what they would be doing. Standing outside waiting for money to go food shopping. It's embarrassing. Shameful, according to some Cree writers. "Years ago our people were self-reliant," writes Harold Cardinal, in *The Unjust Society*. "We made our living by trapping and from whatever nature was able to provide for us. Our life was hard. But we lived like men.... When they offered us welfare, it was as if they had cut our throats."

I move between the queue asking questions. No one wants to talk. I approach a thirtysomething woman in ski sunglasses who is waiting with her three kids, aged twelve, nine, and six. People glance at us as I ask about her welfare. Dipping her head, she cups one hand around her cigarette as she lights. "What choice do we have?" she asks.

Another rush of wet snow stiffens the crowd. I switch focus. About a dozen cars and trucks sit parked, waiting for those in line to collect their cheques. Sheltered by the cabin of their vehicles, the conversations are easier. No one wants to talk about how much they make on their welfare. But shifting the conversation, I find that they are eager to explain the history, and how the high numbers of welfare recipients can be traced back to the origins of the reserve.

Much of Kashechewan's history can best be understood through a series of numbers. The most significant of these, the ones that locals like to talk about, have become smaller. At the start of the twentieth century, the Crees of Kashechewan trapped over 640 square kilometres (400 square miles) over the James Bay area. But in 1905, with the signing of Treaty Nine, they were moved to an area measuring 1.5 kilometres by 0.5 kilometres, the size of the reserve, with 230 kilometres (144 square miles) to be shared among two communities, Fort Albany and Kashechewan, for hunting.

Treaty Nine records the surrender of 144,840 square kilometres of what was Cree land. The Crown got something for nothing, or at least not much. Everyone was given eight dollars per person up front ($169.47 in today's inflation-adjusted currency), and four dollars per person per year afterwards.[1] After signing, the real value of these numbers would shrink too; they weren't indexed to inflation, which became the subject of an ongoing court case filed in September 2014 by the Chiefs of Robinson-Huron Treaty. This was pretty typical for the numbered treaties, agreements between First Nations and the Crown signed across Canada from 1871–1921. They were all modelled on the Robinson Treaty of 1850, which introduced the idea of total surrender of land in exchange for a little money. All provinces signed except for British Columbia, which largely remained treaty free until the late twentieth century.

What the Crees signed was the total surrender of almost all of their land for almost nothing. But what they remember being promised was the sharing of the land and its resources. The two sides would be equal partners in how the land would be used in the future. In exchange, each person would receive some money, but the real investment was in the community. A new reserve would be built with paved roads, schools, and a hospital. Hunters would be given jobs.

Whether the Crown's representatives deliberately deceived the indigenous people is difficult to ascertain — evidence exists on both sides. But one thing is certain — the government didn't make any attempt to clear up any misunderstandings. On asking whether they would be "compelled to live on a reserve," the Crown's commissioners replied that "they could continue to live as they and their forefathers had done."[2] The Crees weren't entirely sure what they were signing in 1905. They were working with translators and the document wasn't translated into written Cree until thirty years after the Treaty was signed.

There are similar tales of false promises with the Ojibwa, Cree, and Anishinabe with Treaty One; Mikisew Cree and Dene with Treaty Eight; the Tlicho with Treaty 11. An ongoing source of tension, it has been the subject of films and books.[3]

Over the past twenty-five years, there have been several court challenges to the terms of these treaties. Some decisions, such as Delgamuukw v. British Columbia (1997), have ruled that First Nations' interpretation of what happened and oral promises made must be taken into consideration when examining who owns the property rights to the land's resources. Others, such as R. v. Horse [1988], have ruled that the treaties must be interpreted like any other document in contract law. What is written must supercede any oral histories or memories. Sadly, today's laws are about as clear as the treaty negotiators. There isn't one principal to decide on the legality and fairness of the treaties; it depends on the judge or the composition of the Supreme Court.

Once the Numbered Treaties were signed, indigenous people were forcibly moved out, and the settlers moved in. In the United States, the same thing had already happened a few years earlier with the Indian Removal Act, signed into law in 1830 by President Andrew Jackson. With that law, Native Americans lost much of the south and east in what is now called Trail of Tears: the Cherokee were pushed from Georgia, the Seminole from Florida, the Choctaw and Chickasaw from Mississippi, and the Muscogee (Creek) from Alabama.

In the United States, after the Indian Removal Act, however, Native American dispossession largely ceased. That wasn't true north of the border: Canada kept going. With the signing of the Numbered Treaties (1871–1921), First Nations had been ejected from their land. As compensation, they had received small plots of land (the reserves), some money, and the promise that they would not be moved again. But the government found that they had allowed too much. Six years after Treaty Nine was signed, an act of Parliament was introduced to undermine those promises. The 1911 Oliver Act allowed towns, cities, and companies to expropriate First Nations land without surrender, so long as the dispossession was used for roads, railways, or other public works. Still, it wasn't enough. That year, the act was further amended to allow a judge to move a reserve for any purpose whatsoever, as long as it was "expedient." Even that was considered too generous. In 1919, the Soldier Settlement Act gave the government the right to forcibly take First Nations land so it could be sold to returning veterans.

One might think that these laws, atavistic and capricious as they are, would have been extinguished long ago, or at least after First Nations were given the vote. A couple of amendments have been made. The Soldier Settlement Act is no more. Soldiers returning home after fighting in battle can no longer seize First Nations land to set up their own farmsteads. But the rest of it — the law that says companies, towns, and cities can seize Aboriginal land, as long as they collaborate with the Ministry — is still on the books under section 35 of the Indian Act. According to said laws, the company or government body doesn't need the First Nation's consent, as long as certain conditions are filled. The Ministry, who sets the price to be paid by the company or government body doing the dispossession, must approve the seizure. The Crown receives the money and decides how and when to distribute to the First Nation.

These laws are not particularly Canadian. In fact, they are very un-Canadian, according to the ideals that we hold, and the principals embodied in our other laws. Section 35 contravenes the spirit, if not the letter of the Canadian Human Rights Act, and several international agreements that Canada has signed, such as the Universal Declaration of Human Rights, and the UN Declaration on the Rights of Indigenous Peoples, which Canada has formally adopted.

These laws also embody the anachronistic values of the time created. When the Oliver Act was signed in 1911, women didn't have the vote, South Asians weren't allowed to become doctors, and it was illegal for gay people to have sex. For First Nations persons, the restrictions were more severe: they weren't allowed to do much of anything. They couldn't hire a lawyer, take a case to court, practise their religion, wear cultural clothing, drink, vote, open a business without a permit, move to a different reserve, or hold political meetings. Legally, they weren't considered responsible adults but "children,"[4] and so they should have the same political rights as kids, which is to say none at all.

The official reason as to why they should be disempowered, the one that was cited in Parliamentary discussions between legislators, was they didn't have the intelligence to be treated as human beings. It was widely believed that they weren't of the same capabilities as "their white brethren," according to the pre-Confederation Legislative Assembly of Upper Canada, and therefore they couldn't take care of themselves, which meant that they weren't worthy of civil rights. "The Indians were excluded from all political rights, the tenure of which depended upon an extent of interest not conferred upon them by the Crown. Their inability to compete with their white brethren debarred them, in great measure, from the enjoyment of civil rights."[5]

Did those in power actually believe this to be true? Certainly, the lesser intelligence theory was publicly accepted, and even discussed in scientific and medical textbooks. But there are also indications that behind the scenes, some realized this was simply a racist power play. For if the Ministry actually believed that First Nations did not have the intelligence to "compete with their white brethren," it would not have been necessary to impose legal legislation that discriminated against them, some of which continues today, such as the anti-business laws. Nor to ban them from taking the government to court when their land was seized. Nor to seize and destroy those Aboriginal businesses that were outperforming their white counterparts, as happened with the Canadian Dakota.[6]

The situation in the United States was a little different. South of the border, indigenous populations were not "wards of the state." According to Chief Justice of the United States John James Marshall, tribes were "domestic dependent nations," which legally required a government-to-government relationship. They were "nations like any other," according to Marshall, which meant firm boundaries and mutual respect. In Worcester v. Georgia (1832), Marshall ruled was that every tribe was "a distinct community, occupying its own territory, with boundaries accurately described."

Here, forced seizure of land was not actually a crime. The Crown owned all the land, even the 0.2 percent that had been set aside for the reserves, and could do with it as it saw fit. "In the United States there has been from time to time question as to the legal status of Indians and Indian land; in Ontario there never has been any doubt that all the land, Indian or otherwise, is the King's, and that Indians are subjects in the same way as others." That was the legal position according to Ontario Supreme court judge William Renwick Riddell. "There are no troublesome subtleties in Canadian law."[7]

In Canada, once First Nations lost 99.8 percent of their land, it became harder to get by. Less land meant fewer animals to hunt. Fewer animals meant less food and less money. For example, hundreds of First Nation communities in Canada were dependent on the bison, as their original range spanned Manitoba, Saskatchewan, Alberta, B.C., Northwest Territories, Yukon, and most of the United States. They stopped hunting the animals when most were killed in the nineteenth century.

The animal skin prices fell too. In 1960, the average price for a large beaver fur was ninety dollars, according to Bobby Wynne, who has six kids and seven grandkids. In 1970, it was eighty dollars. By 1985, it had fallen to thirty-six dollars. "The price went down — it used to pay good," Wynne explains. "Furs is the only way to get money otherwise we are living on welfare."

Mr. Wynne is one of the lucky ones in Kashechewan. His hunting income and store provides him and his family with a valuable safety net. Others are not so fortunate. Some are trapped in a vicious circle. For example, Paul Wesley, fifty, was once known as an expert trapper, a man who could find a herd of moose in a snowstorm. For much of his life, he used to supplement his income by trekking through the nearby spruce forest. He taught all of his five children — four daughters and one son — to fend for themselves in the wilds.

Paul Wesley would like to return to trapping, but he lost his job as a cultural support worker for Health Canada, which means he cannot afford to fix his ATV. The issue is exacerbated by the lack of trees on the reserve. They've been chopped down for firewood. Without vegetation, there are no animals or birds near the community. There's nothing to hunt for miles. To find an animal, one needs a vehicle. Wesley can't trap, so he can't earn any money, which means that he can't afford to fix his wheels, which means that he can't trap.

I met Gemma White, fifty, that day in the welfare line. Like Arthur, she has been unemployed for two years, and has difficulty feeding her children. With fourteen people currently living in her house from three different families, four of her kids currently live with other relatives. What she would really love is a job and a new house, so that she could bring her children back home and feed them something other than canned meat and mac and cheese. Still, she hasn't lost hope. For the past six months, she has attended Faith Temple Pentecostal church to pray for both.

While the people in the welfare line that day didn't necessarily discuss the entire history of how they ended up there, they knew the basics. Treated like children for generations, lied to in order to swindle them of land, moved to a wasteland, and denied all promises of help, many had given up. I would not understand how this despair might cause someone to turn to extreme measures — until I myself was pushed beyond my limits.

SIX

Rumours

To destroy another person's culture is to rob them of immortality.
— Author Temple Grandin

As people are reluctant to talk, or be seen with me, I start to become lonely. I long for my friends and family. I miss water cooler discussions and small talk with strangers. Eager for company, I begin hanging out with children and teenagers who stand around outside the corner shops and smoke.

It is strange for a thirty-one-year-old to be chilling with people less than a third of her age. Even though I am a grown adult who identifies a little too strongly with Peter Pan, it's not something that has happened before or since. But having spent almost three months on the reserve mainly holed up at home, I simply want people to talk to. And if that meant I had to make fart jokes while breathing in second-hand cigarette smoke, then so be it. Besides, there was a theory going around, voiced by the teachers and nurses, that the kids began to become depressed in their teenage years. They started out happy and joyful, and then as they realized what life has in store for them, as they accustomed themselves to ever more lessons in disappointment, they lose that sense of possibility. They begin to become anxious, says Julie Wesley, Kashechewan's addiction counsellor. They "are afraid to dream of a brighter future."

By contrast, Kashechewan's children were responsible for some of my happiest memories of that time. They taught me my first words of Cree.

I learned wonderful terms that have no English equivalent, such as "*tah-wahshin*," which is used to describe that moment when you are walking on frosty muskeg and the ground gives way beneath you. Or "*seekwan*," which means the month that nature renews her promise and the buds open and the geese arrive. Or "*iyihtew*," which refers to the patches of grass or soil that peak through the snow during spring or warm spells.

Sometimes, as my tongue struggled with what seemed like many consonants jumbled together, they would ask how I planned to write about their community without speaking the language. And with each word learned, I would understand a little better what they were driving at, for Cree is a language where the values — like the power of community, the Red Road, and the Seven Sacred Teachings, ideals that are fundamentally different from those of a western, capitalist system — impregnate both vocabulary and syntax.[1]

Hanging about with Kashechewan's children made me happy. They seemed genuinely pleased to see me, and weren't afraid to talk, unlike so many of the adults. They made me laugh and feel liked, and I wanted it to continue which is perhaps why I did something reckless.

On a reserve, even today, Aboriginals have few rights and limited defences. To safeguard the most vulnerable — the children — in a place where there are many stories of abuse, the band council would banish with a BCR anyone believed to be harmful to the community. And for extra protection, kids were not allowed into outsiders' homes.

All this I know. But Emma is gone for a couple of weeks, and I want the company.

In late November, I invite three children who often hang about outside my house — Amy, twelve, Julia, eleven, and Hannah, eight — in for a home-cooked meal.

We eat beef stew — I splurged at the Northern — and play cards. They leave. Trivial, but deeply comforting in its normalcy.

The next day after school they come again. By the fifth day, word of what has happened has reached the high school principal, David Gibb. He knocks on the door. His pursed lips are stretched thin. His eyes dart forward, three paces ahead. We speak in the kitchen.

"Is it true that you are having children come to your house unaccompanied?" he asks.

"Yes."

"Do you know the rules?"

"Yes."

"Stop it. People are starting to talk."

He leaves.

After a week alone, I am standing on the porch of one of the local mom-and-pop stores, zoning out, staring at the stars. It is one of those December nights after a fresh snowfall when the moon gleams and hangs low in the sky. A group of five kids between the ages of eight and fourteen climb the wooden steps.

"Hey Alex," nine-year-old Simon says, smilingly mischievously.

"Hey."

"Are you gay?"

I stare at him. Is this a random question? Or does it have anything to do with my home-cooked meals with Amy, Julia, and Hannah? What are people saying?

"No," I reply.

"Are there gays in Toronto?"

"Yes."

"Lesbians?"

"Yes."

"Have you ever seen any?"

"Maybe. Yeah, I guess."

"Where?"

"Uh. Gay Pride."

"What's that?"

A twelve-year-old girl with flashing eyes and wearing a hoodie answers for me. "It's where they let it all hang out."

Everyone laughs. A few pretend to gag.

"I gotta go," I say, and I run off.

And that would have been the end of it, except that for some reason no one believes my lie, and kids start calling out "lesbian"[2] each time I walk by in the streets.

Looking back on it now, these two events — the rumours of pedophilia and homosexuality — were probably unrelated. That they happened back to back was likely simply a coincidence. Rumours often flew about in Kash. A teenager told me a particularly traumatic tale of the whipping of a twelve-year-old girl, although when I questioned her about it later, she recanted. There are stories about incest, although the main supporting evidence for this claim is that the children in question come to school with glazed eyes, which might be from any number of reasons, including malnutrition or depression.

Some of these stories point to another layer of truth in Kashechewan: the tremendous sense of loss in a place where far too many take their own lives. Three people have said that ghosts of people who have committed suicide haunt the Francine J. Wesley Secondary School. When I ask what the spirits look like — the tall seventeen-year-old Absalom Hughie, known for his "radiant smile," or fourteen-year-old Haven, sweet Haven, a sister to many — they say that they haven't seen their presences, but they can feel their heaviness when they walk the halls.

Rumours spread in times of high stress, according to psychologists. After hurricane Katrina, there were rampant tales, all shocking, and many bizarre: that sharks had infested the waters, terrorists had planted bombs in the levees, and hundreds of armed gang members were killing and raping at will inside the dome, the latter of which was subsequently (falsely) reported as fact by the city's Mayor Ray Nagin. After 9/11, the same phenomenon: fabled rumours included that anthrax had been injected into one out of every five cans of Pepsi, groups of Arabs were caught celebrating the attacks, and Jews were given advance warning and stayed away from the World Trade Centre that day, all of which, needless to write, turned out to be false.[3]

Unlike New York or New Orleans, Kashechewan's population was not stressed by one seismic event. It's not that something terrible happened and then life went back to normal. There have been many things done to the northern Cree population. They were forced to live on a flood plain, went to school at St. Anne's Residential School, a place where children were tortured by electrocution in a homemade electric chair, were the subjects of medical experiments into the effects of malnutrition funded by the government,[4] were gang-raped by residential school staff, and, during the Sixties Scoop, their children were kidnapped and never heard from again. What is normal in such oppressive circumstances is that nothing is too far-fetched to belie comprehension. People are on guard and in search of the next threat.

With the escalating rumours, I start to get drunk every night. First the vodka that I've smuggled onto the reserve, and then, once that has finished, the salted cooking wine that I found in Emma's cupboards. On the night that I run out of booze, I call up Jill. Together we decide that no story is worth my health or this amount of suffering. Tomorrow, I will go to the airport and buy my ticket home. Once I get off the phone, I crawl into bed and sleep like a baby.

The next morning, I awake feeling refreshed. I check the airline, and find out that the flights for the next two days are full. It's not ideal but at least it means that I've got time to pack and say goodbye. On a whim, and since I have nothing better to do, I decide to go to the water plant for one final interview. I have never quit on a story before, and I still can't believe that having spent so much money and having come all this way I will go home with nothing.

It's at the eastern edge of town, sheltered by the dyke, and tucked next to Red Willow Creek. Inside is the control room. It's tidy, spotless, and mould free. Behind a row of monitors sit three men, watching the screens. It smells like chlorine.

A tall man emerges from the tank room. He smiles, and introduces himself as John Gentile.

I tell him that I'm a reporter, and would he mind if I interviewed some of his staff for a story that I'm writing about the water plant and the reserve.

"Oh, Jonathan Solomon told me about you. He said you'd be coming by."

"Really?"

"He seems to like you. I'm not sure what you told him, but he's told us all to co-operate."

Can it really be this easy?

"Do you know anything about the E. coli crisis of 2005?"

"Well, I only started working here in June 2006, so you should probably talk to Alfred Wesley, who was the plant's supervisor at the time. Or Isaiah Wynne, his assistant. Alfred now works as a public works supervisor for the band. Let me call him for you."

An hour later, I am sitting in Alfred's basement. The interview is an important lead.

According to Mr. Wesley, there was indeed a water crisis. They ran out of treatment chemicals for three days — due to shortages. Mr. Wesley is not sure whether or not it caused an outbreak of E. coli. Perhaps, he says, but maybe not. He's not sure. He didn't see any positive proof of the bacteria, such as a notice by Health Canada, but then again, he was away, out hunting, at the crucial period. October is a time of *niskiskou*, Cree for "many geese," when the birds break from their annual migration south and feed and rest along the James Bay coast, and Mr. Wesley was on a two-week holiday. While trapping, he heard that there was an E. coli crisis on the bush radio and made his way back. Once back in Kash, he was told what had happened by Isaiah Wynne.

The interview is surprising. How can he be the former manager of the water plant and not know if there was an E. coli outbreak? I'm about to give up when I tell him Arthur's story about the river water. Ah yes, he's heard the rumour too. Once the correct chemicals had been sent in from neighbouring Moosonee (and the water was clean), it was used as a prop during the meeting with Health Canada, which I later found out also included INAC and took place on October 19, 2005, in the gym of St. Andrew's School. He even knows who from the community went down to Albany to fetch it.

"Was this person from the band council?" I ask.

"No, it was a member of the community."

"Who was he?"

"I know who he was but I don't want to mention his name."

I press, but Mr. Wesley cuts short the interview.

I return to the water plant mulling over what Mr. Wesley has said. The good news is that I now have verification for Arthur's river water story. But the confirmation also creates further questions. If a Kashechewan citizen collected the river water, then either someone from the band council told him or her to do it, or the fact that the water was clean before the Health Canada officials arrived was an open secret, and there were lots of people involved. The latter makes more sense given Arthur's knowledge, but if that's true, then why, after three months of asking people questions, can't I find anyone else who knows what was really going on?

At the plant, I ask Mr. Gentile if it wouldn't be too much of an inconvenience if I worked here for a few hours. I want the company.

"Sure, go ahead," he says. "We'll behave, won't we boys?"

Everyone laughs.

Two hours later, Isaiah Wynne, a man with a tidy moustache and kind, sad eyes, arrives for his shift at the plant. When I ask if I can interview him, he laughs nervously, and suggests that we talk in private at his house a few metres away. We leave and walk around the corner to his home, one of the few on the block that is graffiti free. Since arriving, I've visited a few houses. Most are in rough shape. Black mould patterns the walls. Electrical wires hang loose from ceilings. Holes aerate the floors, walls, and ceilings. Doorknobs, windows, and sometimes whole doors are missing.

Mr. Wynne's is different. Inside polished teak chairs are arranged against a large dining table, and his smooth walls are covered in photos of his children. He's a carpenter, and has built some of the furniture himself. Everything is polished until it gleams.

After making small talk, I take out my recording equipment, and begin to interview him about the 2005 E. coli crisis. This is his story:

While Alfred Wesley was on vacation, Isaiah was the only person on duty. At some point that month, he ran out of chlorine. Afterwards, there may or may not have been E. coli in the water — he answered differently depending on how the question was phrased. He wasn't too sure about dates or details. And he didn't have any records. The "guys" at the "water plant … throw all my papers out … I have to keep my records about ten years. And they threw my papers out, all of them. I don't know why."

I watch Mr. Wynne as he talks. From first appearances he seems like a careful, detail-oriented man. Not someone who would forget key details of a crisis that lasted weeks.

I ask whether he thinks that the crisis was fabricated and carried out to improve the fortunes of the town, and he says "I really can't say anything right now." Why not? I ask. Yesterday, his "boss," who doesn't work at the water plant but at the band council, phoned. He told Wynne not to give "too much information," to "protect us," and "your job." I grill him for more details, and he looks at me apologetically and says he doesn't "know what's going on."

I write down everything he says, and steal a glance at him as he waits for my next question. His eyes dart across the room. I wonder whether this interview puts him in jeopardy in some way. I hope not. He seems like a gentle soul.

SEVEN

Teaching the Children

[On the reserve] history is a story which has no relationship to real life. The entire school curriculum is make-believe, to be deciphered and memorized but not experienced.
— Heather Robertson, author of *Reservations Are for Indians*

My investigations are finally getting somewhere, so I call Jill and say that I'm going to stay.

"How long?"

"Not sure yet."

"I don't like this. I'm really worried about you. What about the homophobia?"

"I've been told that it will blow over."

"When?"

"I don't know. Soon."

"And your drinking?"

"Well, when the homophobia blows over, I'll stop drinking."

"Seriously? That's your answer?"

"Don't stress. I'll be fine."

My glibness is unfair, and we both know it, but I don't want to get into it. Without solutions, talking about the situation makes me feel worse.

———

Later that day, I call Dr. York at his home in Timmins, fishing for any further information. This isn't the first time I've called, but it's been hard to get a hold of him, as he often travels to other northern Ontario communities.

Yes, there was one more thing, he says. Through the grapevine he heard that it was the teachers who had contacted the media. Apparently, they were fed up with the schools' conditions and the lack of infrastructure on the reserve. They wanted more for their students and hoped to give them a better chance in life. Since the government wasn't helping, they decided to take matters into their own hands.

"Who?" I ask.

"Sorry, I don't know," he replies. "But I'm sure that someone knows about it. Ask around!"

The following day, I take his advice.

The high school teaches grades eight through twelve. It's a red brick building that resembles a normal school except for the green shutters that protect the glass from the kids who throw stones. Outside the entrance, students aged fourteen to twenty-four hang about smoking, silent, except for the odd joke. Eight-year-old Hannah, who had dinner at my house, weaves between them, picking up their butts, and putting them in her coat pocket.

My initial plan was to scout the school and find some teachers who were teaching in 2005. It seemed so simple when I thought it up a couple of days ago. But then again, nothing in Kashechewan is ever easy. Most teachers arrive, stay for a few months to a year, then leave again, because they can't handle the stress and are traumatized by the living conditions. With near everything in flux, the students suffer from the lack of continuity. It's hard to build anything when people are just passing through. Bootstrapped projects such as the outdoor skating rink or a third grade breakfast program end as soon as the organizing teacher leaves again. The transience leads to lack of communication.

I walk through the halls. I have a name: Carol Laronde. She is from the Temagami reserve, a small Anishinaabe community, one hundred kilometres north of North Bay. Perhaps because she is First Nation or because she is known as a passionate defender of indigenous rights, she is one of the rare ones who understand the problems faced and still doesn't leave. She has worked in Kashechewan since August 2005.

Walking the halls, it soon becomes obvious why the teachers might have done whatever is necessary to obtain much-needed help. The school has a library, although books are not sorted and instead stacked in piles on the floor. The staff room is covered in papers, pens, and coffee cups. Homemade suicide prevention methods hang from the walls. They ask teachers to look for telltale markers, including "Gathering of Weapons; Preoccupation with Death; Giving away Prized Possessions; Making Final Arrangements." Most students are on daily suicide watch, according to Ruth Stadelmayer, thirty-two, the high school guidance counsellor.

Northern Ontario reserves have already been in the media for having among the world's highest suicide rates. Sadly, as yet, that knowledge hasn't filtered down to policy. Instead of formal instruction, they do their best with whatever they have. When seventh grade teacher Patrick Tucker took his students for a walk past the dyke to Willow Creek, the kids became visibly nervous as soon as they had left the familiarity of the town. Several began to panic. They rarely left the confines of the reserve, an area one and a half by a one-half kilometres large. Given all the things that have been done to this population, children are anxious and have a "siege mentality," he says. It's as if they had grown up in a war zone. That day, he cut the walk short. In subsequent days, to overcome the students' fear and feelings of inferiority, he gave more compliments than usual, and encouraged parents to do the same.

It's not that what Mr. Tucker did was wrong. One could argue that it is admirable. Faced with a lack of help and an absence of resources, he embodies trying to keep going and striving to do one's best, a spirit that is apparent throughout the reserve. It keeps the town functioning, in its piecemeal fashion; it explains why the suicide rate isn't higher than the current reality.

What is hard to comprehend is the disconnect between the amount of help necessary to heal from the after-effects of the residential schools and the reality on the ground. For everything before me has already been carefully recorded in the academic and historic literature. The suicide rates are common knowledge. The panic attacks and anxiety have already been documented in the studies on the legacy of the residential schools. So too have the high levels of self-harm. The lack of training for the teachers is considered a perennial problem. To know and yet choose to do nothing, this is our history, our supposedly moral position.

As I mull over these thoughts, I walk past the gym, where there's an exercise class going on. Several students are staring not at the teacher but at the ceiling fan. I look up. It spins and shoots out sparks. Fortunately, they extinguish a few feet above head height and don't harm anyone. It was the same a few days ago. Asking when it would be fixed, I am told it was top of the school's agenda, and they are trying to find someone with the technical know-how.

No one knows how. I hear that phrase often. It cropped up a few weeks ago when the fuel truck broke down on the way to fill the gas tank that powers our heater, or when explaining why the barely used garbage truck sits idle in the dump, or why there are fire hydrants throughout the town that haven't been connected to the main water supply.

Traditionally, Crees prized self-reliance, a concept they called *bimbo-leytosowin*. The word is richer than the English term, encompassing both a sense of trust in oneself and an innate belief that one can learn how to do anything. In fiction, the best-known example is from Cree bush pilot Will Bird in Joseph Boyden's *Through Black Spruce*. "Lots of times growing up, I'd just try to do something myself because I believed that being a boy, and being Indian, I should just know how to do things."

Today, the loss of this sense of self-belief and the deskilling of the population, the result of both the residential schools and the current education system, creates a sense of stasis. Without electricians, fans throw sparks, wires hang loose from ceilings, and electrical outlets remain broken with their wires exposed. When houses burn down, such as Bobby Wynne's would do, along with his store in March 2012, there's rarely an inquest, and instead usually some debate as to whether it was from a long-ignored electrical fault or arson.

Fire is all around — visible are the shells of burned out vans, cars, or empty lots where houses once existed. There are many stories. In 2002, some kids set alight the local residential school, St. Anne's. Three years later, there was a fire at the Northern Store. The following year, two men died in the prison fire. The next year, St. Andrew's elementary school was burned down. School buses were destroyed by fire in fall of 2006 and September 2008. The water plant manager, John Gentile, lost his Chevy truck to arson in 2008 and later that year the house next door to him burned down. The following year, he lost his garden shed. This has been an issue for the past forty-two years, ever since 1974, when the reserve wrote to the Ministry to ask for the funding for protection, such as a fire department, firefighters, and working trucks. By this year's end, there will be nine cases of arson in Kashechewan,[1] slightly above the yearly average of six, according to NAPs statistics. In a community of 1,800, the problem affects everyone.[2]

Ignoring the fire hazard, I peak into the classrooms looking for Ms. Laronde. The rooms look normal. There are students sitting at desks. But the scene looks strange: the people are big and the chairs small. The students are in their early or mid-twenties. They are old because of death and grief. For example Danielle Koosees, twenty-two, explained that she quit school twice, each for a couple of years, once after her father died of a heart attack, and again after her cousin hanged himself. Harold Moore, twenty-four, stopped because he didn't have anywhere to study. He used to live with his dad, a bootlegger and drug dealer. When he drank, he would beat the boy. Sometimes Harold went to the police, but he was too afraid to tell them what had happened, and so they sent him home again. Aged fifteen, he tried to leave, and his dad strangled him, nearly killing him. Afterward, he dropped out and left home. He drifted between different friends' homes on the reserve. Finally, teacher Chris Mead found out what had happened and offered him a free bed. With a safe lodging, Harold returned to school. He's hoping to graduate this year and go to college.

If he makes it, if nothing goes wrong — his dad doesn't decide to drag him back to his house, the school doesn't burn down, the reserve doesn't flood again, and none of his friends or family commits suicide — then he will earn a small, but well-deserved break: those who graduate from high school have their college tuition paid for by the band. The next challenge will be to stay in college. It won't be easy. The schools in Kashechewan are between three to five years behind their counterparts in the rest of the country. If Harold can play catch up, and he doesn't have PTSD from all the things that he has experienced on the reserve, then there's a good chance that he will be able to achieve his childhood dream. He's always wanted to be a police officer.

Like Harold, most students interviewed said that they hoped to finish high school and go to university. Tyson Wesley, twenty-one, aims to be the next chief. Adrian Metatawabin, twenty-five, wants to go to college and train to become an electrician. Danielle Koosees hopes to become a journalist. It's not a lack of desire. It's that life on the reserve requires almost all of one's emotional and mental resources to stay afloat, explains Julie Wesley. "People go through so much just trying to survive here."

When interviewing elders, such as Paul Wesley, on what's necessary to move forward, he and others point to the past and to the concept of *bimboleytosowin*, which was taught by indigenous teachers. Instilling a sense of self-belief was core to many of the rituals taught to children, including the Walking Out ceremony, where kids who had recently learned to take their first steps "walked out" of their tent through a flap facing the rising sun, dragging a small dead animal behind them, circled a tree, then returned to the tent to give the food back to the elders, symbolizing both their growing independence and the circle of life. Another such ceremony to instill *bimboleytosowin* was Vision Quest, where children aged around eight had to spend one night alone in the bush, while an elder slept a stone's throw away in case they got into trouble. Being solitary in the dark was to teach them how to face their worst fears.

Other rituals taught someone how to stand tall, how to be a good person and have confidence in themselves. Each ritual was designed to teach an ethical code that followed the Cree's Seven Sacred Teachings and the Red Road.[3] When the residential schools were first announced, many indigenous communities, including Kashechewan, assumed that they would be based on similar principals. Children would be taught in an environment of trust and mutual respect. They would learn how to read and write English and Cree. For this reason, many communities initially welcomed them. The Opaskwayak Cree Nation, Manitoba (formerly the Pas Band), petitioned the Superintendent General of Indian Affairs for a residential school, as did the leadership from the Squamish Nation, B.C., and Sweet Grass, the principal chief of the Plains Cree, Treaty Six.

As the years went by, it became increasingly obvious that what was happening in the schools was the antithesis of *bimboleytosowin*. Rather than self-reliance, kids were taught dependency. Dropout rates at the schools were up to 80 percent. There were lessons in regular school subjects — English, math, history, geography, and science, but those teachings were not the focus of the schools. Instead, students became experts at those tasks that had monopolized much of school life: praying, cleaning, and farm work.

Most left the schools without being able to fill in a job application. With sexual and physical abuse common, many finished the schools with PTSD.

Others left the schools in coffins. Death was common. According to Duncan Campbell Scott, Deputy Superintendent of the Department of Indian Affairs, a position that involved supervision of the nation's residential schools, the death rate at some schools was one in two. Illnesses like tuberculosis, measles, and the flu spread easily because of the overcrowding, mould, poor heating, and leaky roofs. Malnutrition was prevalent. It was well known that the kids were fed wilted and sometimes mouldy food, and that they were not given enough to eat. It is likely that the stress of constant physical and sexual abuse also contributed to the high death rates. When children were injured through beatings or rape, there was no medical help. To avoid embarrassment when the children died, the government ceased recording student deaths in 1920 after a damning report by then Chief Medical Officer, Peter Bryce. The Ministry also destroyed 200,000 Indian Affairs files between 1936 and 1944. Which means the official number of children who died in the residential schools — 3,200 — is likely to be an underestimate and the real figure could be between five to ten times higher, according to Justice Murray Sinclair.

It was not the first time that First Nations history had been left out of the official records, either because it was embarrassing, shameful, or wasn't considered important enough. Take for example, the forced sterilization of Aboriginal residential school students in British Columbia between 1933 and 1979. As records have been destroyed, we have no idea of the numbers of kids who were operated on. We know that it happened, because there are stories and anecdotal reports. In neighbouring Alberta, where they kept slightly better records, 2,800 persons were rendered unable to reproduce under the Sexual Sterilization Act, although once again information is missing: this figure does not distinguish by race, and includes non-First Nations also deemed unworthy of becoming parents, such as "mental defectives" and juvenile delinquents.

Or consider the flawed information that exists on the Potlatch laws. The name itself is confusing. The Potlatch refers to a gift-giving feast practised by the indigenous persons of the Pacific Northwest coast of Canada and the United States. Which describes neither the geography nor scope of the repressive legislation. The Potlatch laws were not confined to the

Pacific Northwest, nor were they limited to the Potlatch. Instead, they were nationwide laws that banned all aspects of a person's culture and religion including "Indian dances" outside the bounds of a reserve and "Indian participation" in any "show, exhibition, performance, stampede or pageant" in "Aboriginal costume." How many were arrested for breaking these laws? We don't know. The person making the arrests — the Indian Agent, who acted as prosecutor, defence, judge, and jury — was not obliged to keep records. Scholars estimate that it was hundreds from 1885 through 1951, at which point the laws ceased.

When the government finally began to shut down the schools beginning in the early 1970s, what was supposed to replace them was an education system based on the principals laid out by Indian Control of Indian Education (ICIE), a policy paper created by the National Indian Brotherhood, the precursor to the Assembly of First Nations. Approved by then Minister of Indian Affairs and Northern Development, Jean Chrétien, it became part of the government's official position in 1973. Although written more than forty years ago, it demands many of the same things that First Nations want today. More funding, more control, and a curriculum that is honest about their place in history.

It hasn't happened. Today, schools on reserves receive up to 40 percent less in a place where things cost up to five times as much. To be able to teach, teachers buy school supplies such as pens, paper, and books from their own salary, and transport the supplies in their luggage. Otherwise, the students do without.

Instead of Aboriginal teachers, there are mostly outsiders, usually twentysomethings who are straight out of school. Once they are in Kash, they must handle issues for which they are not trained, such as arson, flooding, self-harm, underage drinking, lack of food, and suicide. And they teach from a curriculum that does not engage First Nations because it barely acknowledges that they exist. Most of the significant events that have happened to the Crees, including the Sixties Scoop, the forced relocations, the civil rights violations, or the systematic impoverishment of the reserve system under the Indian Act, are not taught in schools.[4] None of the students interviewed have heard of the Indian Act, the law that governs the reserves.[5] It is akin to students in South Africa not learning about Apartheid or American students not being informed about the Jim Crow laws.

Arriving in Kashechewan, a fly-in community, for my first visit in September 2010.

Without a fire department, firefighters, or hoses, fires burn long and hard.

Anglicans, Pentecostals, and traditional Cree elders are all buried together in the local cemetery.

These construction workers are doing repair work on a local house.

The main card house in Kash is called "The Poker Shack," where people play Texas hold 'em.

Teacher Chris Mead and his students painted pink hearts on the band office building to cover the graffiti.

Shoot 'em up games are popular among Kash's children.

Although the graveyard is protected by the nearby dyke, it still floods with spring break up.

One of several Native-run stores on the reserve. The Indian Act's restrictions make it difficult for local businesses to make money.

Inside a local snack store. The cost of goods at the Native-run stores are much cheaper than at the Northern, sometimes the same price as in Toronto.

Without a playground, Kashechewan's kids still find ways to have fun. "Shagging" is a game where kids glide along the ice, hanging off the back of a moving vehicle.

First fishing trip on the Albany River.

Me with twelve-year-old Ariel, who dances a mean hip hop.

The neighbourhood kids loved this trampoline. The teepee in the background is a place to chill or smoke wild meat.

After a day spent wandering the school, I find out that, contrary to what I've initially been told, Carol teaches at the elementary, not the high school. I leave and walk there.

In the old St. Andrew's Elementary School, mould was discovered in 2005. The building was evacuated and sat empty for two years, then was burned down in 2007, likely an arson attack. Afterwards, the government imported eleven blue bungalows, known as "portables," which were supposed to be a temporary measure until the money surfaced for a rebuild. Everyone is still waiting.

At the school's entrance, the twentysomething receptionist asks who I am and what I am doing there. I explain that I'm writing about Kashechewan and that I'd like to interview some of the teachers.

"I'll have to clear it with the principal, Judy Stevens," she says.

Judy appears a few minutes later.

"No, that will not be possible," she says. Neither the board nor the parents have given permission.

I thank her and walk home.

For the next couple of days, I do little other than email Carol Laronde while holed up in my broom closet room. The kids are still calling out homophobic names.

As it makes me anxious, and I have run out of everything else to drink, I have started buying two-hundred-dollar bottles of vodka from the local bootlegger, a very nice man named Peter, who knows that I am broke and sometimes gives me discounts. Occasionally, the thought flits through my mind that I am developing a serious problem. But I dismiss it. I'm not that type of person, I reassure myself.

When I finally meet Carol Laronde, fifty-four, at her home, she insists that whatever the historic record, the water crisis was genuine.

Prior to the crisis, the reserve was in a bad way. It was worse than today. The homes were overcrowded and children were sleeping in shifts. The water was on permanent boil water advisory and had been for two years.

Health Canada issued an E. coli warning on October 14, 2005. In response, several teachers, including herself and the band council, sent out press releases to the media. They spent hours looking up numbers in the phone book, handwriting faxes, and contacting dozens of news media outlets. That's how they managed to get the reserve noticed. "It was important to get the word out about what was happening in Kash," she says.

She doesn't mention anything about the river water story. What was brought to the crucial meeting with Health Canada and INAC on October 19 at St. Andrew's School were jars of tap water.

I ask Ms. Laronde whether she has any extra information, and she tells me that she compiled a folder and CD of how it all happened. It's at her home in Temagami First Nation. When she returns for the Christmas holidays, she'll collect it. If I can hang tight, all will be revealed.

EIGHT

The Double Standard

You have to start with a healthy home. It's hard to think of economic development when children are dying and old ladies are sick from the lack of running water.
— Former Westbank First Nation Chief, Ron Derrickson[1]

The reserve is making me sick. Skin diseases are more common here, from the dust, diet, stress, and sleeping on bare mattresses on the floor. Although they affect life 24-7, in general, they are kept hidden. It's winter and people dress warmly. In the whole time since arriving, I've only seen the one woman at the Northern who had a rash on her arms. She was scratching in the pasta section.

I wouldn't have given this incident much thought, except that a couple of months later, I develop my own rash on my chest, resembling a rosy leopard print. Googling it, I find out it's ringworm. At the Northern Store, I buy an over-the-counter cream, which does not make much of a difference, despite my applying it religiously. This condition, which despite the name is not caused by worms but by fungi, should not upset me as much as it does. It's not life-threatening, nor is it particularly debilitating. It's itchy and slightly unsightly. That's it.

More problematic is my asthma, which has flared up, causing breathing difficulties at slight irritations, or if I try to do anything more strenuous than a leisurely walk.

I am not alone, according to Dr. York. The dust from the unpaved roads and the dirt from the overcrowded houses causes the lung problems. As does the mould that I have seen in several houses. Kashechewan isn't an isolated case. On Canadian reserves, one in two houses are contaminated with mould, according to a 2012 *Journal of Environmental Health* study.[2]

At first, I complain about these minor health problems to anyone who will listen. But after a couple of weeks, I start to feel foolish. Whining about asthma and ringworm makes me realize how good I have it. Nothing that has happened to me can possibly compare to what locals deal with daily. Cornelius Hughie, twenty-eight, says he can't afford to feed his four-year-old daughter. Addiction counsellor Julie Wesley explains that she still has panic attacks from being sexually abused by her uncle when she was nine. Arthur White explains that he can't afford to eat properly and it is making him tired.

Even those who are based here for a few months without a break can crack under the stress. For example, Emma has started waking up in the night moaning. Evenings, she uses her SAD lamp and has stopped cooking because she's too tired. A local nurse, Jake Arbus from Petit Codiac, New Brunswick, twenty-nine, says that not being able to better help his patients has made him depressed, which he believes has aggravated a flare-up of diverticulitis. A police officer explains that his colleague has become moody and twitchy. Teacher Ruth Stadelmayer has developed irritable bowel syndrome since arriving, which she believes is from the frustration and anxiety of dealing with children from unsafe homes, and trying to set up a safe house for victims of domestic violence. She raised the issue with several band council leaders, but it didn't get very far: there is no spare space in any of the buildings, and when she offered her own home to persons fleeing violence, it was too stressful.

Although these individual cases have not yet been reported, the issue of burnout is familiar to anyone with a passing knowledge of the reserves. Forty percent of the full-time nursing positions in the Sioux Lookout First Nations Health Authority are vacant, according to Mae Katt, an Ojibwa nurse based in Thunder Bay who specializes in First Nations health. All fifteen of the Oji-Cree communities in northern Ontario have trouble finding teachers, school principals, and nursing staff to work in their communities, and once they are there, convincing them to stay becomes another hurdle, according to Judy Finlay, an associate professor in the School of Child and Youth Care at Ryerson University.

We've even created systems so people who work on reserves do not catch whatever illnesses the locals have. Outsiders employed in isolated communities are given plenty of time away. Like those working dangerous jobs such as in a coal mine or as a firefighter, we, the outsiders, are on rotation. The cops stay for sixteen days; then leave for twelve. The water plant operators and managers work for two weeks, then home again for the same length of time. The nurses choose their own schedules, but it's usually about three weeks on, then away for a week or two. The Anglican minister returns home about every two months. The teachers do the same.

It would be hard to argue that rotating people on and off the reserve, despite the enormous expense, is not a good thing. Consider the alternative: Patients seen by nurses too worn out to give the right prescription. Water filled with bacteria because its plant manager is burned out and doesn't add the right chemicals. A cop who fails to take accurate notes because he is exhausted. Protection of one's health is necessary. But it also seems like the ultimate band-aid solution. Rather than change the conditions on the reserves, we ensure that the outsiders who are flown in to do the jobs that require professional qualifications — the ones that locals are excluded from by the failing education system — don't collapse from being here too long. Aboriginals are second-class citizens, even on their own reserves.

Having discovered that compared to everyone else, my health problems are minor, I stop telling everyone my woes. However, I still need to be well in order to continue functioning. There aren't any doctors in Kashechewan as Dr. York won't be back in town for another three weeks. So I call up a physician friend of mine, Lindsay MacMillan. We chat for an hour or so and I tell her my problems. She says I am right to be worried, but my experiences are not totally unexpected. I ask her how she knows. She tells me her story about coming to Kashechewan and becoming involved in the crisis. That's when I get my first real break. And ironically, it's from someone whom I've known for years and lives a ten-minute bicycle ride from my Toronto apartment, a friend who is now one thousand kilometres away.

It started with a phone call on October 21, 2005, from her supervisor, Dr. Trusler, Chief of Staff at Weeneebayko General Hospital, Moosonee, Ontario, where she was doing a one-month residency. Had she heard about the water crisis in nearby Kashechewan? She had. People were sick, he said. It was an emergency and the Kashechewan leadership had asked for his help. Could she come with him?

The next morning, she, Dr. Trusler, and a research assistant named David Bowen flew to the reserve by helicopter and were met by a member of the band council. They were driven to a row of houses at the centre of town and began going door to door, looking for symptoms of E. coli. There were none. Two things were immediately apparent. First, no one was suffering from the symptoms that had been discussed in all the newspapers. Second, even if the water was drinkable, and the E. coli crisis was fabricated, people were still sick.

Touring the houses, what struck her were the kids. They were living in dilapidated conditions that were making them ill. In Kashechewan's children, there were lung problems at extreme rates. She treated toddlers with pneumonia and six-month-old babies with asthma. Beyond lung problems were the skin conditions. People were sleeping on floors and in sheds, which meant that personal hygiene was near impossible. Many kids had some form of skin disease, such as ringworm, scabies, or impetigo, she said.

The two doctors took photos of what they saw. And they did their best to treat these conditions, handing out prescriptions, antibiotics, and anti-fungal creams. But several of the diseases witnessed that day could not be solved in a single visit, including the chronic conditions such as heart disease, high blood pressure, diabetes, and stroke. They required a change of lifestyle and long-term care, near impossible given the diet and the lack of any facilities to keep fit. "People are forced to eat unhealthy, poor quality food," she said. "That's the tragedy of it."

That the conditions on reserves are rundown enough to make people sick has become an uncomfortable familiarity. In the past decade, there have been several studies confirming it. Diabetes rates are three to five times higher, according to Health Canada.[3] Self-reported obesity rates are double that of the general population, according to Health Canada.[4] Other diseases related to an immune system weakened by stress and poor diet are more common too. Some First Nations communities have infant mortality rates up to four times higher than the Canadian average.[5] HIV rates are ten times higher on reserves than in the rest of the country. Tuberculosis rates are thirty-four times higher on reserves than in the general population. Public Health Emergencies, such as the one declared by several Northern Ontario First Nations' communities on February 24, 2016, have become common.[6]

Some deaths on reserves are considered noteworthy. Others don't register at all. They matter to husbands, wives, friends, and family, but not to the general public. To the external world, diabetes on an impoverished First Nations reserve is not unusual; it is to be expected. Same with suicide. Hardly a week goes by without a report of a reserve struggling with another cluster of deaths. However, if the same person had died of E. coli poisoning, it would likely become front-page news.

Neither of us knows for certain why this is happening, but we both offer our own theories. Dr. MacMillan believes that it's to do with solvability. The general public views many issues on reserves as intractable. Without solutions, people feel disempowered so they tune them out. Water, though, is viewed as a different type of problem as it's considered fixable without needing massive investment or changing the basic structure of reserves. If we can do something but choose to do nothing, then the issue is not money or lack of resources. It says as much about us as the situation.

I agree. But I also believe a death by E. coli is considered more important than a suicide because of how we assess who is ultimately responsible. If you drink water that contains E. coli and die, it's definitely not your fault. Somebody must be held accountable. But if you hang yourself, then at some level you've made a personal choice. There's no one to blame. For this reason, suicide on First Nations reserves is considered less of a problem than poisoned water.

Admittedly, my argument starts to disintegrate under scrutiny. No one actually thinks that a nine-year-old makes a perfectly rational choice when they attempt suicide. Or that a person chooses to be sick. *I'll have the diabetes please. Yes, type 1. Early onset.* And yet, through the many studies and the many discussions of those studies, at some level we've rationalized why our reserves have the world's highest suicide rates. We find it acceptable that in a nation of plenty, one of a handful of countries that is a net exporter of food, one race of people goes hungry.

Dr. MacMillan believes that any story on the water crisis must address these issues and discuss how the reserve's conditions are causing health problems. She also believes that the band council used the issue of bad water to address the real issues, which is that the reserves are so rundown that they are making people sick. We discuss it some more, and then I tell her that I'm going to find someone to interview who knows for certain.

Until now, I've interviewed many people in the town — residents, teachers, nurses, water plant officials, and band councillors — and what I have gained is fragments, tiny pieces of the story that sometimes contradict each other. I need someone to weave them all together, a person who will clear up for me whether or not the band was perpetrating a hoax. I hope that if I just keep asking questions, I'll eventually get somewhere. A couple of days after my conversation with Dr. MacMillan, I find someone from Kashechewan's leadership who is willing to go on record.

His name is John Koosees. In October 2005, he was "water crisis coordinator," which involved discussing and helping shape the leadership's response. I never found out why he agreed to go on record. But I had met him a couple of days earlier at a community function, and he had said that he had tried many things to help Kashechewan's children, including working as a youth counsellor, addiction counsellor, and as a crisis worker, but it was hard to get anywhere because the situation was overwhelming and daunting and, as a result, many people "don't want to know."

Which is how I found myself at his office at the western edge of town. I climb the wooden steps and knock.

"Come in!" a male voice shouts.

A man with eyes as bright as a crow greets me with a firm handshake. He's about five feet eight inches and ripped. He leads me through the lobby and we both sit down at his desk. Taking out my recording equipment, I ask him about the water crisis. Drawing a breath, he tells me what happened.

Before the water crisis, Kashechewan was in a bad state. The overcrowded conditions were causing health problems, he says. Kashechewan's health director, Edward Sutherland, tried to raise awareness of what was happening by writing reports and sending them to the appropriate authorities, but nothing happened.

E. coli was discovered in the water on October 14, 2005.[7] At first no one paid much attention. Yes, there had been an outbreak of deadly bacteria in a First Nations water supply. But so what? (There were already seventy-five thousand First Nations people living with undrinkable water. It was hard to get anyone to care.)

Still something had to be done. The community could not continue living with the high levels of sickness. Parents could not stand back and watch their children commit suicide. So Edward Sutherland contacted Dr. Trusler. He was known to be a passionate defender of First Nations rights, someone who had a reputation for going out of his way to help.

This is when Dr. MacMillan, Dr. Trusler, and Mr. Bowen flew into the town and went from house to house taking photos of the overcrowded conditions, the sickness, blocked toilets, and the mould. Afterwards, the pictures of skin diseases were sent to the media and blamed on the E. coli, according to Dr. MacMillan.

But was it a hoax? I grill him on this subject but we don't get anywhere. I've got a little valuable information, but nothing like what I had hoped for. Another promising lead is fast becoming a dead end.

Instead, the conversation turns, as it often does, to suicide. Managing the reserve's epidemic is now his full-time job. All of his counselling clients are children under sixteen. He begins to tell me about some of them. By the end of the year, there will have been thirty-four attempts. Pills, hangings, slashing of wrists. I frantically scribble but I cannot keep up. After an hour, my interview time is over and it's time for me to go. Mr. Koosees leans back and sighs. I glance at him and he offers a sad half-smile, stands, and shows me out.

NINE

Comparisons

Tell a person long enough and often enough that he is inferior, and likely he will eventually accept the false image you thrust upon him.

— Cree activist and author Harold Cardinal

Mr. Koosees's interview stayed with me; it still haunts me now. It seems obvious to me that a parent could not stand and watch their kids dying — could not remain trapped with no way out — without wanting to do something drastic. I want this idea to have merit, to connect it to everything else that I have learned about the reserve and figure out how all these little pieces can be pulled together to explain what really happened in October 2005, but none of Kashechewan's leadership is telling me what I need. Instead, I file some Access to Information requests and I wait.

In the meantime, the reserve is in the middle of a suicide crisis. Two weeks ago a fifteen-year-old girl tried to kill herself by taking a rope and putting it around her neck and then attaching it to the tallest thing that she could find in her bedroom. The girl's father found her before the rope got too tight, thank God, and then did what always happens when someone tries to kill themselves: medevacked them to the nearest hospital with an open bed, which, in this case, was Timmins. The date was significant — it was on the night before the anniversary of the successful suicide of a fourteen-year-old girl from Kashechewan the previous year. Many are worried that the attempt will trigger other kids and there will be a cluster.

Suicide attempts are not rare in this tiny community of 1,800. There will be 34 by the time the year ends.[1] On average, there are 16.2 per year, according to NAPs statistics. Then there are the pacts. In January 2007, a suicide pact formed between 21 people, mainly children and some as young as 9. They overdosed on pills. Fortunately, they were found before the drugs were fatal. That same month, there was another pact among girls aged nine to twelve. In the summer of 2006, a group of seven seventh-graders, five girls and two boys, tried to kill themselves again with pill overdoses in the girls' bathroom of their school.

After the latest attempt, the teachers decide to look out for anyone who is acting strangely or talking about wanting to die. We are all told to keep our eyes peeled. It isn't much as a suicide strategy, but it's better than doing nothing. That's how I found myself listening in on the conversation of a group of six children between ages nine and fourteen standing on the porch of one of the corner stores on a Saturday night. I am trying to be discreet, but Tom, a gregarious boy of nine, notices that I'm eavesdropping.

"Alex." Pause. "Have you ever suicided yourself?"

"What?" I ask. *Did he read my thoughts?*

He pretends his hands are a noose and mock strangles himself.

He asks again: "Have you ever suicided yourself?"

I am surprised. Tom is considered a pretty happy-go-lucky boy.

"No," I reply.

"Why not?"

"Because I like life."

"She has," he says, pointing to Kristal. She's a skinny kid of fourteen. I look at her. She doesn't look depressed. Instead, everything about her seems handled with loving care: it is hard to stay clean in Kashechewan because of the dust and yet her clothes — checked jacket and skinny jeans — are spotless.

She glares at Tom. "No, I haven't," she replies.

"Yes, she has," he adds.

As if to prove him wrong, Kristal rolls up her jacket and shows me her right arm. Four purple scars run its width. They look like they were done with a razor. Is it suicide or cutting? It's hard to say.

"Where did you do that?" I ask.

"In my parents' bedroom."

"Does anyone know?"

"No. I've been doing it for a while, but I don't tell anyone."

"Come on," Tom says. "Let's go."

I watch them descend the stairs. I want to do something, but there's nothing to do. It isn't suicide, but self-harm. An estimated one in four children either cut or burn themselves, according to teachers. It's a way of numbing the internal pain of living on a troubled reserve. While a cry for help, it is not an imminent threat to one's life, which means that it's not an acute crisis. As a result, there's no immediate assistance. Suicides are given top priority — there's crisis coordinator Karen Wynne and John Koosees — but for cutting, the student has to wait for one of counsellor Joan Barker's monthly visits or, even longer, for six months to get into an in-treatment addiction program off-reserve.

Before arriving, I thought that there would be lots of help for the children who were impacted by the legacy of the residential schools. My assumption was based on Prime Minister Stephen Harper's 2008 apology. On June 11th of that year, he stood in the House of Commons and said, "The government now recognizes that the consequences of the Indian Residential Schools policy were profoundly negative and that this policy has had a lasting and damaging impact on Aboriginal culture, heritage and language." He promised that the government would move "towards healing, reconciliation and resolution," and take "a positive step in forging a new relationship between Aboriginal peoples and other Canadians."

Those promises lasted a couple of years, but healing and reconciliation turned out to be expensive. In March 2010, citing budget cuts, traditional healing programs and the organization running them, the Aboriginal Healing Foundation, began to close before they had a chance to reach troubled communities such as Kashechewan. In cities nationwide, people protested these closures. In Montreal, demonstrators held up signs saying, "Stop the Attack on Native Communities," "500 Years on Stolen Native Land," and "Apology? Hypocrisy!" In Ottawa, a sit-in outside Minister of Indian Affairs Chuck Strahl's office led to the arrest of six protestors. They were led away and that was that.

It wasn't the first time that the Crees of Kashechewan had been promised help only to see those commitments abandoned. In late 2005, in the wake of the water crisis, when the nation was watching the reserve, the leadership asked for help dealing with their record-high suicide rates. In one of the few times throughout their history, perhaps because the public was interested after media coverage about their bad water, they got exactly what they requested. Ottawa promised to "enhance counselling, psychological supports and youth outreach" for their community and others in the region and to "enhance family violence and suicide prevention services throughout the area."

When I ask what happened to these promises, the answer is unexpectedly generous. "You know politicians; they tend to say stuff and then after they leave, they tend to forget," explained Kashechewan's former health director, Edward Sutherland, who now worked as a resource and land use coordinator. Mr. Sutherland is keen to give those who have forgotten their promises to this troubled community the benefit of the doubt.

Without external resources, the band council has implemented its own suicide prevention schemes. In October, there was a town-wide suicide prevention walk. Occasionally, there are suicide prevention nights organized by John Koosees. In the fall, Karen Wynne put out a call for suicide prevention volunteers, although no one has come forward as yet, according to Kashechewan nurse Scott Miller.

Most interviewed believe that these programs are starting to help, although the suicide issue will not abate until people can support themselves and access jobs. The lack of employment makes it near impossible to survive on the reserve, but also near impossible to leave. I met Meredith White, forty-eight, a few days after she had collected her welfare cheque. She had been unemployed for two years, and explained how hard she tried to find work on her reserve — trying at the band council, the two schools, and the nursing station. There was nothing.

Thankfully though, her husband had a job at Kashechewan Power Corporation, the local hydroelectric distribution company, meaning she could at least afford to feed her seven children, though barely. Things came to a head in 2009 when she walked in on her depressed fifteen-year-old-daughter Janine trying to hang herself in her bedroom. Meredith rushed her to the local nursing station, and they medevacked her to Timmins. While in hospital, Janine saw a psychologist. She seemed to improve. The whole family rejoiced.

At the time of Janine's attempt, Kashechewan was already known to have a suicide problem; it had been freely discussed in the media ever since those twenty-one people formed a pact in 2007. Suicide rates in Kash were estimated to be 2.5 people per year by the fly-in coroner, which, in a community of 1,800 people, made them twelve times higher than the national average and higher than any other country in the world. Given its national and international reputation, Meredith presumed the help would continue once Janine returned to the reserve two weeks later.

Returning home, Meredith petitioned the nursing station for help, but there wasn't any funding. Janine couldn't get the medical care she needed. When she slipped into another depression, Meredith moved the whole family to North Bay, minus her husband, who was still working at the power company. But off the reserve, she soon found that her sporadic employment history made her virtually unemployable. After a year of job hunting for entry-level positions in places such as Walmart, she had spent all her savings and returned to the reserve. "We tried," she said and shrugged her shoulders when telling me her story.

Many First Nations leaders, including former Fort Albany Chief Abraham Metatawabin (leader in the mid-60s) and Mr. Reuben, espouse the link between suicide and employment. In support, they point to the genesis of the problem: until the 1960s, the idea of suicide did not exist for the Crees. There was no word for it. No one did it, or at least not in numbers that it impregnated the community's consciousness enough for it to become a concept. But in the decade when First Nations received the vote, people began to take their own lives. It wasn't the voting that caused it. In becoming citizens, the government began to take more interest in Aboriginal populations, and introduced more social policies to shape behaviour.

These changes aimed at settling nomadic hunters into a nine-to-five life. More houses were built that decade to encourage people to stop roaming and settle down. To sweeten the program, provincial governments introduced welfare programs across the nation, such as Ontario's 1965 Indian Welfare Agreement, which were implemented either biweekly or monthly. As people needed to be near the welfare office to collect payment, long trips on the land were no longer possible. The Crees and other First Nations had to abandon what was often described as a hardscrabble, but independent and rewarding existence. "Years ago our people were self-reliant," wrote Harold Cardinal. "We made our living by trapping and from whatever nature was able to provide for us. Our life was hard. But we lived like men. Only a man who was crazy would go out to work or trap and face the hardships of making a living when all he had to do was sit at home and receive the food, and all he needed to live."[2]

As it has become harder to get by, and more people have turned from autonomy to welfare, many First Nations writers, such as Harold Cardinal, Howard Adams, and Calvin Helin, have written about how what initially seems like free money is actually a prison of free thought and the soul. Welfare is not a free lunch, for what is bought is autonomy and independence. It is payment for co-operation, for one's silence. "It is not so much the giving as the implication," writes Harold Cardinal in *The Unjust Society*. "When that man looks at you as he hands over the check and you reach for it, you know what it means. It means that you aren't man enough to make your own living, it means that you aren't man enough to feed and clothe and house your own wife and children. That's when an Indian hates welfare."[3]

Once the welfare rates rose, several government policies made it difficult to leave dependency. The relocations have moved First Nations away from resource-rich areas, such as fishing, forestry, mining, oil, and natural gas. Their traditional economies have collapsed with these relocations, and the modern alternative has been successively squashed by lack of investment in the reserves, and with the anti-business provisions in the Indian Act.

Several studies have found that these directly relate to the suicide rate. Probably the best known is by Ronet Bachman, an American sociologist who examined the link between poverty and suicide in her 1992 book *Death and Violence on the Reservation: Homicide, Family Violence, and Suicide in American Indian Populations.*[4] Comparing reservations in the United States, Bachman found family violence was the biggest predictor of suicide. If there's been a murder in the home, you're more likely to kill yourself. After that, the biggest predictors are poverty and unemployment. Reserves with the highest unemployment are those with the highest suicide rates. This is for a range of reasons. Not having anything to do or anywhere to go upon waking each morning. The poor health that comes with not being able to afford fresh vegetables. Not being able to buy clothes or toys for your kids. Being unable to leave the reserve. The loss of meaning. The shame.

After Ms. Bachman published her work, her findings were then published and quoted in the 1996 Royal Commission Report on Aboriginal Peoples, which used them to recommend many changes to help enrich and empower First Nations. In part, these changes would improve people's lives, but they would also help to lower the suicide rates, which the report said were extremely high, although it would be four years before they became known in the Canadian media as the world's highest.[5] Unfortunately, the RCAP faced the same fate as many such reports and studies of Aboriginal persons. Most of its recommendations were not implemented; and the high suicide rates remain.

Among Native youth who live on reserves, the mean suicide rates are five to seven times higher than the Canadian average. In remote communities, the numbers are higher still. In Kashechewan, the suicide rate is estimated to be twelve times higher than the national average. In Pikangikum Ontario, the rate is thirty-six times the national average.[6] The Ontario Oji-Cree community of Neskantaga's rate was ninety-six times the national average from 2013 to 2014, although during these two years, the only ones for which we have records, there were several clusters in the community, which elevated the baseline rate.

If Bachman is right, we might expect these communities to be desperately poor — and they are. Kashechewan's unemployment rate is the previously mentioned 86 percent, Pikangikum's unemployment rate is 90 percent, Neskantaga's is 85 percent. Which means that the average salary in each of these places, averaging both those who work and those on welfare, is similar to Kashechewan's of $9,741 per person in a place where a bunch of grapes costs $13.42. It is difficult to put food on the table, let alone leave the reserve to try to find work.

Although it is difficult to establish whether this link between poverty and suicide holds across all reserves in Canada (most don't calculate their yearly suicide rates, and income statistics and unemployment rates are missing from many Statistics Canada First Nations profiles), it is possible to compare averages across nations. In Canada, the suicide rate on reserves is 65 to 91 per 100,000, or five to seven times higher than the national average. The median income for First Nations people living on a reserve is fourteen thousand dollars,[7] compared to thirty-three thousand dollars for everyone else, or less than half. By contrast, in the United States, the Native

American youth suicide rate is 22.5 per 100,000, or twice the national average.[8] There, the median household income on reservations is $38,583 ($29,097 US) compared to $55,684 ($41,994 US) nationally.[9] Native Americans earn 69 percent of the average salary. The cross-border comparison is not only a national embarrassment, but supports Bachman's theory.

These numbers are important both because of what they say about poverty and what they indicate about income inequality. It isn't just that Canadian First Nations are poor. It's their relative poverty compared to other Canadians. That's the finding of many studies, including a 2008 British study by Anne E. Kazak and others.[10] Examining 40,400 adults, she found that income status was the biggest predictor for well-being. People are happier when they feel that they were doing pretty well compared to their peers. It doesn't much matter who does badly or well, so long as others are in the same boat.

This issue surfaced often in conversation in Kashechewan. When discussing the suicide rates or poverty, a couple of phrases cropped up time and again. "I can't believe this is Canada!" or "we live in one of the world's richest countries and this is on our doorstep." What frustrates isn't only the Third-World poverty but how it compares to Canada's abundant wealth. That our reserves lack fresh food or clean water is bad enough, but even more jarring, is that we live in a country that consistently ranks as in the top ten in the Human Development Index.

Many First Nations leaders have tried to change this situation. The first, or at least the first in recorded history, was Frederick Ogilvie Loft, a Mohawk from the Six Nations of the Grand River Reserve, who served as a lieutenant in the First World War. After seven years of service, he returned to a country where First Nations did not have the right to vote, and had over the past forty years been dispossessed of most of their land with the signing of the Numbered Treaties. To stop the loss of First Nations land and raise the conditions on the reserves, Loft's League of Indians was born, the first national Aboriginal political organization in Canada.

It was a historic moment, but the victory was short-lived. Ottawa ignored all his communications, and declared the League to be a bunch of communists, similar to The International Workers of the World (IWW), the One Big Union, or other such "Balshevick [sic]"[11] organizations. Loft was nothing more than a cash-hungry opportunist who got "them [First Nations] worked up about … their grievances."[12]

Determined not to back down, Loft organized meetings in reserves across the nation and wrote articles and gave interviews to the *Globe*, *Saturday Night*, and *Toronto Star Weekly*. As the government isolated him further, he left the country, then fell ill and died. Some reports say the cause of death was partly ostracization and overwork.

Loft was the first, but this tale of people raising the alarm bells, of giving their all to change the conditions on the reserve but finding themselves consistently stymied, is not unusual in First Nations history. One could argue, and many have, that it is the norm. It was the fate of Kashechewan's chiefs Andrew Reuben, Dan Koosees, and Willie Wesley. Beyond Kashechewan, it was the story of former Fort Albany Chief Abraham Metatawabin, Mohawk Chief Joseph Onasakenrat, and former National Chief of Assembly of First Nations Shawn Atleo. Each of these people fought for better living conditions on their reserves — non-mouldy houses, fire protection for their homes, affordable food, and safe drinking water — but faced countless setbacks. Of all these leaders, only those from one community managed to raise sufficient public sympathy to change their destiny. Unfortunately, to accomplish these aims, it was necessary to embellish the truth.

TEN

When the Waters Rush In

You see we are up against so much ... there was a time until the fifties that we survived.... But then the big machinery came and it displaced us.... The logging trucks destroyed our traplines. After machinery came welfare.[1]

— Mary John, elder of the Stoney Creek
Indian Band, British Columbia

I still need Carol Laronde's CD to complete my investigations, but I can't live here much longer. My body is breaking down, with the lung and skin issues. I believe that the dermatological and pulmonary issues are connected somehow, but am uncertain about what to do with this knowledge. It's not clear who can help. Most people are already stressed out.

I sleep only with pills and vodka. With booze, many things are more manageable on the reserve. I don't mind that I live in a broom closet without a door. The homophobia rolls off my back. The constant noise becomes bearable, as do the aggressive stray dogs, and seeing the burning, cutting, and suicide scars on children's arms.

Some nights, I abstain. That I can do without offers a welcome, if brief, semblance of self-control, but those sleepless nights are worse. The next morning, I am groggy and anxious. I make mistakes. Usually, only small ones, thank God. For example, the other day I deleted a ninety-minute interview I did with Edward Sutherland. Now I have to persuade him to agree to be reinterviewed, which in a place where no one picks up the phone or answers messages, won't be easy.

Other times, my slip-ups are large. For example, I dropped my house keys in the snow. I didn't realize until I reached into my pocket at the doorstep.

"For fuck's sake!" I screamed. I began to pound the door.

There were a couple of children, two girls, an eight- and nine-year-old, playing with the snow in the ditch outside.

"Did you swear at my friend Rosie?" asked the nine-year-old.

"No," I replied. "I swore, but not at Rosie."

"You swore at Rosie. I heard."

"No, I didn't."

Rather than explaining myself, I ran off.

I find it difficult to assess the severity of what is happening. My rapid mood swings are not ideal, but I've been told that accepting the unexpected is crucial to surviving on a northern reserve. So too is managing a higher level of risk. And yes, I need chemical aids to stay calm and sleep, but at least I am moderately functional the following day. As Jill, my family, and friends have questioned my ability to cope in Kaschechewan, and evidence has mounted for the contrary, the one belief that has sustained me is that I can, at least somewhat adequately, perform my job. I have clung to this idea, as the conditions on the reserve have chipped away at other tenets of self-belief: I am a balanced, resilient person; I do not overreact; I have good coping skills. A new-found lead in my investigations this week supports what has now become the flimsiest of lifelines — that despite mentally and physically falling apart, I can turn on my recording equipment and ask coherent questions.

I have discovered that what happened in 2005 was not the reserve's only E. coli outbreak; there was another the following year at the start of spring. However, unlike the first outbreak, the second received almost zero coverage. There was nothing reported on it in either the *Toronto Star* or the *Globe and Mail*. Since any radio story on Kashechewan must explore how and why a crisis becomes international news, I am curious why the first instance of E. coli caused mass panic, while the same event the following year barely scratched public consciousness. I am trying to set up some interviews on this subject, when I fortuitously meet

Julie Wesley at the nursing station, where she works, having recently
returned from taking courses at Northern College in Timmins. She has
straight jet-black hair pulled into a neat ponytail, soft eyes, and a mouth
quick to smile. Beyond her work as an addiction counsellor, she's also
a community leader, sitting on several of Kashechewan's committees,
including the Kashechewan powwow, James Bay Mental Health, and
Kashechewan Youth Leadership.

It turns out that we have a mutual friend. Andrew Wesley, a Cree elder
who has helped me on other stories about indigenous issues, and now lives
in Toronto, is an acquaintance. Perhaps for this reason, she agrees to talk
after work two days later.

As the sun slips behind the clouds, I take a taxi to her house, passing the signless video shop, Philip's store, and the spot where, three
weeks previously, one of the teachers broke her leg after falling on
the unsalted, icy roads. Visible from the car window is a roof where
four dogs, a lab and three mutts, lie frozen. They have been shot and
placed there so the wolves don't eat them. They won't be buried until
springtime when the ground unfreezes. I have been told to expect
more canines killed as flooding season approaches. It's considered a
compassionate way to end their suffering — the dogs will likely starve
if the reserve floods.

On arrival, I pay the taxi cab driver four dollars and knock. She opens
the door. Her eyes are puffy.

"You all right?" I ask.

"Not really."

She hasn't slept much. For the past few nights, she has had night-
mares about the reserve flooding and awaking in freezing water unable
to breathe.

Flooding is an aspect of reserve life like suicide or bad food: it is
ever-present and impossible to avoid. Every year, there was a possibility
that their homes would be washed away or flooded with sewage. The constant threat meant it was almost impossible to build successful businesses
or convince private industry to invest in the reserve.

Technically, the town is supposed to be evacuated each year before
the flooding happens. To figure out the likelihood of flooding, each day
a band council representative measures the river's height at three spots

on the Albany. Measurements of water velocity and thickness of ice and snow are collected daily and sent to the Ministry. The department decides whether the numbers warrant an evacuation. But due to cost cutting, any evacuation is left to the last possible minute. Evacuating 1,800 people by plane out of a place without roads usually takes two weeks. Which might be fine if the river wasn't erratic. With the effects of the tides, snow buildup, and spring melt, the water can rise five metres (fifteen feet) in one day. But the dyke itself is only nine metres tall, (thirty feet) and is, according to an outside consultant Hatch (an engineering management company), at an "intolerable risk" of collapse.

Inside Julie's house, we perch on chairs in the kitchen next to piles of toys, clothes, and dishes that are stacked on the table, kitchen counter, and every available surface. There is no room to put anything away with ten kids and four adults living in the three-bedroom house. Blushing, she apologizes for the overcrowding and the mess, so I change the subject, asking about the 2005 water crisis. Unfortunately, she doesn't know anything — she was living in Timmins at the time. But she answers my other questions: the reason why the media didn't pay attention to the 2006 E. coli outbreak was circumstance and cause; it was not instigated by mistakes at the local water plant, but by the spring break up that flooded the plant. By then, Kash was a ghost town — most people had already been evacuated.

I explain my difficulties in getting people to talk. She sympathizes. The people of Kashechewan have been through a lot, she says. Terrible things have been done to her people for generations. The only thing I can do is keep going. And it might help having a local person vouching for me. If I like, she says, she could be that person. She'll message people through Facebook tonight.

I thank her. As I leave, she gives me a list of names and numbers of people to contact, including Kashechewan's flooding coordinator Enoch Williams and Edward Sutherland. Since the latter's name has already surfaced a few times in conversations about the water crisis, I decide to take a taxi there.

A few blocks from his office, I see a group of four boys aged about fifteen wearing parkas standing in the middle of the road. They watch a twelve-year-old girl named Jane about twenty metres away. Her look catches my eye: like a starling caught by a hawk. Staring at them intently, she fiddles with her rucksack. I've met Jane several times at community functions such as funerals and the Thanksgiving feast. She reminds me of myself at that age: she dreams of being a writer, and her favourite book is Harry Potter. I look at the boys again. The scene turns fuzzy for a split second, until I realize that the girl has been hit by a stone. She bolts.

It's the third time I've seen this happen — kids throwing stones at each other. What surprises is the speed: the sudden movement as the perpetrator reaches down, grabs and tosses a rock, the victim bolting or trying not to flinch, and just as suddenly, the outburst of repressed anger is over, and everyone behaves as they do with all Kashechewan's crises, whether it's a suicide, arson attack, or a flood, what people do when there is a serious problem and no help, which is trying their best to pretend it never occurred.

We arrive at the band office. Edward Sutherland's office is in the basement. I walk past the perennial mopper, and head downstairs.

Mr. Sutherland smiles and then shakes my hand firmly. He asks what I think of Kash. *It's fine*, I reply.

We start to talk about the reserve's flooding. It's been an issue since 1957. That summer, an Indian Agent flew to where the community used to be located: two adjacent islands, Sinclair and Anderson, and began to visit families in their log houses and tents. He recommended that the reserve move to a more convenient location nearer to the Hudson's Bay store. Residents did not want to. They pointed out that his suggested location was about as thoughtless as they come: located at the centre of a bowl-shaped depression, the lowest point for an estimated 150 kilometres squared. It was at the confluence of four waterways: the Albany River, Yellow Creek, Chicknick Channel, and Stomping River. It was known to flood.

Two months after the Indian Agent first arrived, they still had not moved, so Ottawa sent in the RCMP. They went without a fuss to some marshland five hundred metres away. The Ministry issued a new name for their reserve, a misspelled version of *Keeshechewan*, which in Cree means "where the water flows fast." The soggy location and botched translation became Kashechewan.

Predictably, once relocated to the flood plain, the waters began to rise. The first major recorded flood was on April 26, 1976, and was reported in both the *Toronto Star* and the *Globe and Mail*. Residents were stranded on ice mounds, as large ice shards from the overflowing Albany ripped through their homes. They huddled together in minus-six-degree weather, the waters rising, waiting to be evacuated by helicopter. No one had the time to rescue their possessions. "All that was left in the village were some dogs and cats as helicopters began searching nearby areas for any other people who may have been marooned by the surging waters," according to the April 26th front page of the *Toronto Star*. "The town's entire population, estimated between 600 to 800, was airlifted by helicopters to Fort Albany, 10 miles to the south ... there is no way of telling when they will be able to get back," according to an article two days later in the *Globe*.

After that, the flooding became more frequent, the result of population growth, global warming, and deforestation. In 2010, the flooding was estimated to happen about once every four years. Today, it happens nearly every year.

Whether this relocation was legal, let alone moral, is open to debate. Eleven years earlier, in 1948, Canada had signed the Universal Declaration of Human Rights. Much of that document was designed to prevent things that have happened in Kashechewan. The forcible removal of persons is forbidden by several of the Act's rights and freedoms, including:

Article 3: Everyone has the right to life, liberty and security of person;

Article 7: All are equal before the law and are entitled without any discrimination to equal protection of the law;

Article 17: No one shall be arbitrarily deprived of his property.

But at the time that Kashechewan was relocated, everyone went to a residential school. Which meant that they spent their days doing farm work and praying — they weren't taught about subjects such as the law and the United Nations. Most people didn't have any idea that the UN even existed, explained Reuben when I pressed him about it later, let alone that Canada had signed an agreement that might offer them legal protection. Nor could they take the matter to their political representative. They didn't have any — they weren't allowed to vote. (Canada was a holdout on this front, enfranchising its First Nations population in 1960. In the United States, indigenous people got the vote in 1924. In New Zealand, the Māoris won this right in 1867.)

While they might in theory have been able to return to their original land once the Indian Agent had gone, in practice, no one would dare. Consider the legal environment when they were relocated: they had about as many rights as a black person under Apartheid, which is to say, not many at all. The Indian Agent, who flew to the reserve every three to four months, had near absolute power over their lives. It was he who decided where a person should live; where they could trap; whether they have visitors to the reserve; whether or not a person could open a business, what they should sell, how much, and at what price; whether they could move house; and what the correct punishment should be if a parent did not send their children to residential school.

With so little under their control, many were uncertain about their rights. Most assumed that whatever the Ministry did, no matter how unjust it felt, was above board and there wasn't legal recourse to protest, says Andrew Wesley, an elder who was born near Kashechewan, and considers neighbouring Fort Albany his home. "We did what they said because we were afraid that they would fly-in, arrest us, and lock us up."

In such a legal environment, it was easy to displace indigenous persons, even if it negated the promises made with the Numbered Treaties of the nineteenth century and the 1763 Royal Proclamation. And it was easy to continue moving First Nations persons around, as if they were unwanted bedroom furniture, long past the era of Herbert Spencer's Survival of the Fittest and nineteenth-century colonial expansion, and into the late twentieth century. This is where Canadian history differs from that of other developed countries, such as the United States and New Zealand, which also committed mass displacement of their indigenous populations, but mostly stopped after the nineteenth century. As a result, Canadian First Nations have less land compared to those in other developed countries. For example, in the United States, Native Americans account for 2 percent of the population and reserves comprise of 2.3 percent of the total land. In New Zealand, Māoris account for 14.6 percent of the population, and own 5.5 percent of the country. By contrast, Canadian Aboriginals make up 4.3 percent of Canada's total population, while reserves account for 0.2 percent of the nation. This although Canada is an underpopulated, sprawling country near the size of a continent, with a land mass slightly larger than the size of the United States, and a population one-tenth the size.

Some Canadian Aboriginal communities were first relocated in the early twentieth century. They were given assurances about honouring their traditional land and never being moved again, but then relocated multiple times; for example, the Keewatin Inuit, the Mi'kmaq at Nova Scotia, the Hebron Inuit, the Mushuau Innu, the Inuit at Ennadai Lake. Some First Nations were moved to places that were considered uninhabitable and left there, for example, the Crees of Kashechewan were moved to a flood plain and the Oujé-Bougomou Crees were moved to a swamp.[2] The Gwa'Sala people were forcibly relocated from Takush village on the coast of Vancouver Island to three houses in Port Hardy with twenty to thirty people per dwelling. Since it wasn't possible to fit thirty people in each government allocated house, they tried to move back. The government burned down their former homes.

There's a banality to evil, as Hannah Arendt has said, but even so, the procedural thoughtlessness of these relocations is exemplary. Take, for example, the Sayisi Dene (meaning "people of the east" in their language Chipewyan), who now live in Northern Manitoba. In 1956, the Ministry decided that the Sayisi Dene were not getting enough to eat and therefore needed to be moved. (In fact, they were, but the department had miscounted the number of caribou in the herds.) The spot chosen, just outside of Churchill, Manitoba, named "Camp 10," was a rocky, windy outcrop measuring three hundred by six hundred feet, devoid of any trees, sanitation, or fresh water, and only accessible by foot. And it was located next to a cemetery. The Sayisi Dene believe living near the dead tempts evil spirits, that it is blasphemy. Nights, people began reporting the sight of ghosts walking around the camp. Sewage and garbage began to accumulate about the town. Days, people went hungry. Children found food by scavenging in the local dump. Dumpster diving was seen as necessary but highly dangerous, as Camp 10 was located in the polar bear migration path. Within five years, an estimated one-third of the original Sayisi Dene population had died from disease and malnutrition.

Or there's the Mushuau Innu. In 1948, the government decided that they should be relocated from their homes at Davis Inlet to a new location called Nutak in northern Labrador. The reason, the government said, was the caribou were dying out (again, they miscounted). Without consultation, they were loaded onto boats and transported two hundred kilometres to a location lacking trees and hunting. Hunger and alcoholism spiked. After a little over a year, the Mushuau Innu decided they were fed up, and migrated back. In 1967, Ottawa tried to repeat that ill-fated social engineering experiment, once again without consultation or planning. The Mushuau Innu were again loaded onto boats and moved to a new site, Iluikoyak Island, on the east cost of Labrador, which was remarkably similar to Camp 10. It too was located on a rocky outcrop without running water and it lacked hunting. It was believed that the Innu would simply shift from hunting caribou to becoming full-time fishermen, not because they had any desire or proclivities for their new profession, but because the new site "was not too far from fishing grounds." The rock was considered too expensive to dig, so houses were built without sewage systems. Waste and garbage began to accumulate. On January 28, 1993, Canadians were jolted into an awareness of the effects of such policies when a video was released of a group of children as young as nine high on gas. Several of them were screaming, "I want to die. I want to kill myself." Adult unemployment was 80 percent. Three-quarters of the population were said to be alcoholics.

While anecdotal reports abound, it's unclear how many of Canada's relocations were handled like the Sayisi Dene, and caused people to die in large numbers. There haven't been any comparative studies on the effects of indigenous relocations. Information on Canadian indigenous history is often missing, sometimes deliberately so. But what we do know is pretty damning. For example, in the twenty years of research on community dispossession all of the studies have found that those relocated suffered from PTSD. All of the relocations have impacted people's ability to hunt and financially survive according to the past two decades of research.[3] What's more, in every community we know about, the extreme trauma has led to self-harm.[4]

After Kashechewan was forcibly relocated to a flood plain, the community began to petition the Ministry for solutions. The first, in 1987, was for the replantation of the trees next to the Albany. The vegetation would act as a buffer for the rising ice and aerate the soil. The plan was turned down; it's unclear why as the explanation offered — "does not meet criteria for funding" — was characteristically vague, and the Ministry would not release any information on the subject despite my emails. After six floods, each costing an estimated fifteen million dollars in evacuation costs, the winds of fortune changed. In 1996, Kashechewan received its first protection from the Albany's floodwaters, a six-million-dollar clay and gravel dyke. From the beginning, it had several problems: it was a cheaper version than the type requested by the First Nation, and it did not have the shallow slopes that help slow flood waters with increased drag. Ottawa did not provide funds for the dyke's maintenance, and the local community did not know how to maintain the flood protection gates. With the extreme northern temperatures, they soon fell apart. The year after the dyke was built, the community flooded again. As the reserve continued to flood, the community turned to other measures to save their community: in 2004, the local government asked for one hundred thousand dollars to rebuild the community's culverts to quickly drain the reserve of excess water and reduce the damage to infrastructure. The Ministry said no. In 2005, the worsening floods meant culverts alone could no longer drain the reserve, and the reserve requested $250,000 to repair the sewage and drainage system. The Ministry said that there wasn't the money. Today, those solutions are no longer considered adequate, as the flooding problem has worsened year upon year.

While the historic mistakes mount, our legal system is structured such that the Ministry has the political equivalent of a get-out-of-jail-free card. For while the government decides when and where to relocate people, and whether or not to give them flooding protection, that's where their responsibilities end. They aren't required to deal with the consequences or solve the problem. Legally, the Ministry isn't responsible for emergency management on the reserves. The Aboriginal leadership is given money, albeit not enough, and told to run their communities efficiently by "prioritizing their spending." The First Nation decides how to allocate the limited funds, whether to spend them on hunger relief or coping with the ongoing child suicide epidemic, for example. It's a mirage of decision-making power that gives them the legal responsibility when anything goes wrong, such as fires, flooding, overcrowding, or toxic mould. They have all the responsibility and no money to cope.

How does any of this relate to the water crisis? Well, in October 2005, for the first time in their history, with the nation watching, Ottawa promised that the flooding would end once and for all, as the community would be moved to higher ground. Ottawa made that promise after a presentation by Dr. Trusler to Premier Dalton McGuinty on October 25, 2005, at Queen's Park. We don't know what was said in that meeting, but according to Mr. Sutherland, inviting Dr. Trusler to the community was the brainchild of Kashechewan's leadership, a "core group of people" that included then Deputy Chief Rebecca Friday, Chief Leo Friday, water crisis coordinator John Koosees, St. Andrew's elementary school principal Lloyd McDonald, and teacher Carol Laronde. They met almost every day at the nursing station, the band office, or the elementary school during the crisis to discuss "how to get Health Canada to step in and help. And also how to get fresh water. How we could help the community. And whether we protest or not, all that stuff."

I press Mr. Sutherland on whether the core group engineered a hoax. He insists they didn't. Instead, he says that in October 2005, there was an E. coli outbreak that caused people to have diarrhea, stomach aches, and a sudden outbreak of skin rashes. In response, the core group invited Dr. Trusler to town, and he brought Dr. MacMillan and research assistant David Bowen.

My interviews are beginning to feel like the Japanese film *Rashomon*. What I have is dramatically different versions of the same event and pieces of a story that rarely line up. It is easy to feel frustrated, but while sitting there, my recording equipment in hand, mired in confusion, I notice something. Whoever is doing the retelling, whether Kashechewan's former health director Edward Sutherland, water crisis coordinator John Koosees, teacher Carol Laronde, or then water plant supervisor Alfred Wesley, people smile when explaining their version of events. Their voices quicken. At a distance, it looks like hope.

ELEVEN

A Call for Help

We are in a state of shock. When is enough? It is sad. Waiting is not an option any more. We have to do something.[1]

— Jonathan Solomon

By mid-December, I am near breaking point. When I try to examine what is wrong, unwanted images flash rapidly before my eyes: children stumbling outside the high school drugged out and in pain, teenagers' forearms covered in the yellow craters of cigarette burns, Harold showing me scars on his skull where his father beat him. I don't want to look any more. I don't want to see.

It is snowing. The winds outside whip up the white flakes on this bitterly cold afternoon so walking feels like traipsing through a sandstorm. Thankfully, I am inside at twenty-nine-year-old Jared Bruce's house. I have started interviewing people like him not because I believe that their story is related to my investigations, but simply to keep busy and avoid being alone with my thoughts. Jared is unemployed, but like nearly everyone I have met, is searching for a job. With his roommate out, he is giving me a tour of his two-bedroom bungalow, showing me the spots of black mould in his bedroom and bathroom. It's common on the reserve because of the frequent flooding. I take a couple of photos to illustrate it as part of my reporting, but they don't come out very well as the lighting isn't great — just a dim bare bulb hanging from the ceiling.

We finish the interview and I sit on his couch. I begin wondering how long it will take for someone living in a house full of mould to develop lung problems.

"Do you like wine?" he asks, interrupting my thoughts.

"Sure."

"Red or white?"

"It depends on the type."

He stares at me.

"You know, a Cabernet Sauvignon, a Merlot."

He shakes his head. *Why would he know these wine types? He's living on what is supposed to be a dry reserve.*

"Red, I guess."

"My friend says he can get some. I was wondering if you wanted to come over on the weekend."

"Thanks, but I, uhh, I don't want to drink on the job."

His eyes momentarily narrowed.

"Are you using me?"

"Huh?"

"Using me for my story? So that you can become famous."

I look at him blankly. I'm a journalist. Why else would I be here if not for his story?

I mutter something about wanting to do the right thing. No one says anything for a few moments. He starts to tell me about his niece who had set fire to the curtains and burned down her aunt's house, but I tune out. I am distracted and confused. I don't understand what he meant by "using me," or why he is talking to me if he doesn't want to be written about. A few minutes later, I leave.

Something happened between me leaving that afternoon and that night that I shall never know. Perhaps he spoke to someone who said I wasn't to be trusted. Or maybe he was still dealing with the intergenerational legacy of the residential schools. (His parents had gone to Bishop Horden residential school, which was like St. Anne's, a lawless and violent place, and were dealing with their own legacy of emotional and physical abuse.) Or perhaps he simply became angry at not being able to find work and living on a flood plain with a house full of mould.

That night, he sends several inappropriate messages to my Facebook account such as "races like u bitch's don;t belong in ourrlives,we know better" [*sic*]. I ignore them.

The next day, there are more messages. That night, he comes to my house. Thankfully I am not home at the time, but Emma says he is looking for me.

I call the police and hear a beeping noise. The line is engaged. There are seven part-time officers, rotating on and off the reserve, and all doing shift work, which means that there's usually only one person on duty, according to Kashechewan senior constable Raymond Sutherland. There is also only one phone line for the detachment so when an officer makes a call or two people dial simultaneously, the line is busy.

Moreover, there is more crime. The number of drug offences is 12 per year per 1,800 people, or 2.3 times higher than in Toronto, according to NAPs statistics. The number of break and entries is 30 per year or 4.3 higher than Ontario's capital. The number of assaults is 145 per person per year in Kashechewan or 8 times higher than in Toronto.

Waiting by the phone, I compare my situation to that of the Kashechewan Crees. I think about all the people who haven't been able to get help when they really need it. There was Harold who hadn't been able to find a safe place to live, and as a result, his dad had almost killed him. And Cornelius Hughie who couldn't find a job and was worried about being able to heat his home and feed his four-year-old daughter. And Meredith White who hadn't been able to find any help for her daughter when she tried to hang herself.

When I think of Jared, I imagine everything that might go wrong. In him, I place my biggest fears about life in Kashechewan, a story that has been repeated throughout history: that in a time of crisis, one would call out, plead with the right people, but no one would come.

I feel anxious. I need air. Leaving, I walk down the snowy streets past the sign-less video store and the wooden shack where people play poker.

The police station is at the edge of town. It's a grey bungalow building. In the yard sits a GMC grey Safari missing most of its windows and covered in broken glass. I walk past it and try the station's door handle. It's locked. I walk around the building shouting out "hello!"

No one answers. I lean against the building, waiting. After ten minutes, I walk home.

That night, I try to sleep, but cannot. At 4:00 a.m., I drink a couple of glasses of my bootlegged vodka, take three sleeping pills, and drift into a fragile sleep.

Over the next few days, I don't tell Jill or my family what is going on. They are upset that I am still living on the reserve after I explain some of the dangers, including the arson problem, lack of fire department, and overwhelmed police service. When I complain to them, and hear their worry and fear, it makes me feel worse.

Rather than speak freely, I begin tuning out. I stop leaving my house, except to go to the Northern. I cancel interviews. I drink heavily.

The situation appears to die down by the end of the week. Jared's messages stop, and he ceases coming to my house. But I cannot let it go.

How dare he think he could bully me into dating him? And why the fuck does he dare to show up at my house?

Things come to a head after what happens with Natalie. It's a cloudy Saturday night and one week after Jared had shown up at my house. The street lights are dimmed as usual in Kashechewan, presumably to save money on electricity. I have ventured out of the house to try to start interviewing people again. I have seen a group of five girls around the ages of twelve to fifteen, standing around outside the skating rink, smoking and laughing.

As I walk by, one of them, thirteen-year-old Natalie, a non-smoker wearing an oversized black parka, steps away from the group and towards me.

"Alex," she says. "I'm lonely. I need a hug."

Poor thing. Me too.

Instinctively, I step forward. My arms encircle her body. She starts to shake.

She's crying.

I look up at the rest of her friends. Two have their hands over their mouths. I look for sympathy and tenderness. But the creases around their eyes are turned upwards.

They are smirking. Why?

I see the scene through their eyes. It looks like a lesbian in a romantic embrace with a child.

I look down at Natalie. *She's not crying but laughing. They're framing you.*

Panic sweeps through me. My arms loosen. And then outrage. I remember the angry notes from Jared, being chased by stray dogs, watching children being stoned, kids calling out "lesbian" outside my house, and the fruitless walk to the police station.

Prickly currents of rage jolt through my arms. I grab Natalie, pinning her arms to her sides. Then I push.

She is lying in the snow with her eyes closed.

I stare at her. *What have I done? Oh, fuck.*

She opens her eyes and her body jolts with life. "You bitch," she hisses.

"You cunt!" shouts out one of her friends.

"Sorry," I say, stepping towards her. I kneel down offering my hand.

She grabs my scarf and it tightens around my neck. I begin to choke.

I grasp it with both hands and pull as hard as I can. She releases the scarf and I fall back.

I look up. Three teachers, two women and a man, all in their twenties, are standing on the other side of her group of friends. I hurry towards them. They encircle me protectively.

"I didn't mean to; it wasn't my fault; she was trying to trick me." My excuses run together.

A twenty-five-year-old named David speaks.

"They were playing a prank. It wasn't your fault."

I glance at him. From his look of surprise, I can't tell whether he really believes what he is saying or is just trying to make me feel better.

"Am I going to be okay?" I ask. He raises one eyebrow.

"People are going to talk."

"What will happen?"

"I don't know. But they'll be angry."

"What should I do?"

"You should go."

Two days later I buy a plane ticket and leave the reserve.

TWELVE

Moral Injury

*We get frustrated and scared. We don't give a damn what happens
to anybody any more because nobody gives a damn about us. The
only thing we know is to cause trouble and go to jail, where you
have three meals a day and a place to sleep and a TV to look at.*
— Stan Sinclair, a Métis from Moose Lake in northwestern
Manitoba, who has been in and out of prison
for sixteen of his twenty-six years alive[1]

Back in my Toronto apartment, I simply try to pretend that none of
this has occurred. In my head, I am home now, and everything will be
fine. Besides, I can't quite believe what has happened. I have never hit
or pushed a child before. That isn't me. It's as if I have discovered that
underneath everything I know and like about myself is a strange thing,
cruel and uncontrollable. I want nothing to do with that self. I wish to
forget it is even there.

In general, I am pretty successful at my deception. I have written
down what has happened in my diary, but I do not look at it again. Nor
do I mention it to anyone. Out of sight, out of mind.

My black dogs appear at night. I find it difficult to doze off. When I
do, I wake up screaming. And I cry a lot, especially when I unexpectedly
remember those we have most failed: the children. I don't understand
what is happening, so I say little, and when I speak, I downplay what has

transpired. Instead I chalk it up to the difficulties of acclimatization. I have already been warned that I won't be myself for a few weeks, that it would take time to adjust moving from a place where people are just trying to survive to one of abundant wealth.

I haven't finished the interviews, nor do I have Carol's CD, so I need to return to Kashechewan, but I put off the story. When questioned about why I left suddenly or am postponing my plans for return, I say that I am tired and need a break. Which is true. Living on the reserve has taken a toll on my health. I have gained weight, my asthma has worsened, and I have acne on my face and back, and ringworm over my chest. For the early part of 2011, I focus on getting well again, eating well, working out, and going for long walks.

As my physical health improves, I begin to question what happened with Natalie. My recollection is so out of sync with my values and ideals, not to mention regular life, that the incident has an air of unreality. Maybe my memories are exaggerated or I dreamed the whole thing up. Or perhaps if I can convince myself that it hadn't actually happened and manage to forget then others would too.

The mind is a strange thing, and while this deceit becomes increasingly draining and convoluted to maintain, it allows me to continue with my original plan to return to the reserve.

It isn't just the interviews and the story that drive me on. Part of me desperately wants to make amends. I hope to prove to myself and others that I am not the swearing, aggressive, violent person who had left the reserve. I fantasize about asking Natalie for forgiveness, and then going further, helping Emma with her school breakfast program, importing school supplies for the children, and finding a lawyer for Harold who might help him expunge the criminal record that he obtained while drug dealing for his dad so that he can achieve his childhood dream of becoming a police officer.

I return in the middle of flooding season. Arriving from the airport, I take a taxi into town. Boarded up houses drift past. Smashed vodka bottles litter the ditch. A thirtysomething man walks past an icy yard covered with scraps of toilet paper, like tiny crumpled white flags. We drive on and a skinny man in his early forties, who's swaying as he walks, steps in front of the car. We swerve. He doesn't seem to notice, so focused is he on not slipping on the ice. Drinking spikes every flooding season, according to Julie Wesley. It's a way of coping with the anxiety that comes with being trapped on a flood plain without a proper drainage system or pumps and with the floodgates in a state of disrepair.

After settling in, I head to the skating rink where I had last seen Natalie. I'm told that she's gone to Kapuskasing, a town two hours northwest of Timmins, until flooding season is over. It seems that she and her friends have kept mum about what happened because no one says anything to me about it or looks like they know what has happened. I am relieved, but it does not assuage my guilt.

And so I set about scheduling interviews. I have little success. It is difficult to be back. First, people cancel on me. No one has time to talk. They are too busy boarding up their houses and stockpiling food. A few are sealing their possessions in plastic because when the water plant floods, the untreated sewage can inundate the town.

And I am distracted. I can't seem to let go of what happened in December. Each time I see Jared's house, I panic. Passing the police station, I remember that fear-fuelled night and I have to turn back. The skating rink reminds me of Natalie and I am filled with guilt. I had returned with high hopes but I find myself doing little other than sleeping late and staying home, afraid of leaving the house. I collect Carol's CD, but otherwise, I am not able to do any of the things that I had planned.

On the day before I leave, I bump into Chief Solomon. He is sitting in a black SUV near Faith Temple Church. His window is rolled down. He waves at me.

"So you came back," he says.

"Err … yes." I stare at him, wondering if he has heard about what happened with Natalie.

"For flooding season?"

"Yes."

He smiles. "That's good. It's good that you will see what my people have to go through every year."

With that he drives off.

After leaving an impoverished reserve there is said to be a period of adjustment. It goes by different names, including decompression time and culture shock. Many Aboriginals need time to find their feet and the resources to retrain. Given the high levels of joblessness on isolated reserves, many don't have much of an employment history. For them to financially survive off the reserve, they need to quickly find a way of supporting themselves that isn't hunting or welfare: an employment program or full-time, all-expenses-paid education.

Others may require emotional supports. Many have suffered twice, both from the legacy of a history of violence against them, and the lack of supports on the reserves to address that present manifestation of past wrongs, whether PTSD, the breakdown of families, or sexual, physical, and domestic abuse. A study that examined the toxic legacy of the residential schools involving seven reserves in Northern Manitoba reported that over 70 percent of the women and 50 percent of the men claimed they had been either physically or sexually abused.[2] In some northern Aboriginal communities, it is believed that between 75 percent and 90 percent of women are battered.[3]

All this we know. And yet despite all the ink spilled, the studies and government reports, regardless of the mea culpas and apologies, most receive the same help as Meredith White when she tried to leave her reserve. None at all.

The results of this travesty are all around us: the racialized poverty, murdered and missing women, high levels of Aboriginal persons who end up homeless, world's highest youth suicide rates, the police brutality, and the growing problem of trafficking indigenous women and children.

These realities not only violate our ideals, but are cause for alarm and action. Our First Nations live in Fourth World poverty. We have the world's highest suicide rates for any community studied, Native or non-. An estimated seventy-five thousand people live without drinking water. We know that human trafficking of indigenous women and children is an issue, but do not monitor how widespread it is, nor have a national coordinating body to prevent it. For this reason, we are often criticized on our record on indigenous issues by many international organizations, including Amnesty International, Human Rights Watch, and the United Nations.

These serious social issues were not my fate. As a non-Aboriginal person, I am infinitely better off. Back in my Toronto apartment, I can return to my everyday life, and with it, tap into the supports necessary to regain my health after the trauma of living on a troubled reserve. I have my family, my girlfriend, friends, my own apartment, and a family doctor, Dr. Shirley Epstein, who soon realizes that something is seriously wrong.

At first, she thinks that it is an issue with my lungs. I am tired all the time, weak and short of breath. After a blood test, I am diagnosed with tuberculosis. According to a 2013 report by Public Health Agency of Canada, the rates on reserves are on average thirty-four times higher than in the rest of Canada, and on isolated northern communities, higher still. It's due to the lack of health care and dilapidated houses, half of which are contaminated with mould. Dr. Epstein and I theorize together: I must have been exposed to the disease while interviewing people who were sick.

No one told me that they had tuberculosis, either because they didn't know or they were embarrassed. This is not unusual. A Statistics Canada study published in 2009 found that First Nations tended to underreport their health problems. It's a coping mechanism: there isn't much medical care.[4] If there's no help, many think it's better not to know.

One week later, a chest X-ray reveals that the disease is latent. Everyone, including Jill and my family, is relieved. The disease is noncontagious and can be treated immediately with antibiotics. With the diagnosis, another issue arises. Latent TB should be symptomless. Which means the other symptoms that had begun on the reserve, but continue in Toronto — panic attacks, flashbacks, mood swings, anxiety, depression — cannot be explained away through the white plague.

In those early meetings, I do not tell Dr. Epstein all that is happening. I am embarrassed by my inability to cope on the reserve. I am ashamed that I started to drink heavily, and continue even now, as I flirt with death by mixing my alcohol with sleeping pills. I do not know how to deal with these feelings, so I try to downplay what is happening. Time heals all wounds, as the cliché goes, and I believe that if I just continue with my normal life, eat healthily, and exercise regularly, the memories will lessen, as will my guilt. Everything will be fine.

As days turn to weeks, and then to months, without me returning to work, it becomes increasingly obvious that I need psychiatric help. Although I downplay my symptoms, all those closest to me — Jill, my parents, and friends — are anxious about what is going on.

In July, Dr. Epstein diagnoses me with PTSD.

According to the manual of psychiatric disorders, the DSM-5, PTSD is caused by "history of exposure to a traumatic event," which causes a series of symptoms including "intrusion [unwanted thoughts], avoidance, negative alterations in cognitions and mood, and alterations in arousal and reactivity." The triggering event is usually a form of extreme trauma, such as rape, war, horrific car crash, or being a victim of or witnessing sexual abuse. How the incident is handled can also play a role. A breach in our moral code makes it more likely, according to US Veteran Affairs psychiatrist Jonathan Shay, author of *Achilles in Vietnam: Combat Trauma and the Undoing of Character*. "Veterans can usually recover from horror, fear, and grief once they return to civilian life, so long as 'what's right' has not also been violated."[5] If soldiers have fought wars where people have been tortured or non-combatants have been killed without consequences, people find it hard to justify what has happened and what they have done. Mental breakdown is more likely.

I have not killed or tortured anyone, but I feel guilty about how I had behaved on the reserve. Beyond my individual guilt, I feel my part of a collective sense of responsibility for what we as non-Natives have done to the people of Kashechewan, and to Aboriginal populations in general. We are guilty of a cultural genocide. We have covered up our wrongdoings. "What's right" has been violated many times.

Thirty minutes later I leave Dr. Epstein's office with a prescription for antidepressants, sleeping pills, and a referral to a psychiatrist. I decide to be proactive, and while waiting for the specialist appointment, I take an eight-week mindfulness course. It gives me a lifeline, and I am able to return to work. I am not able to finish the CBC documentary because it proves impossible to complete the interviews in Toronto. No one picks up the phone in Kash. And my heart just isn't in it. Any mention of trauma still gives me flashbacks. Instead, I focus on light, lifestyle stories, becoming a consultant for an American health and wellness website. A month goes by. A year. Two.

I intended to put my time in Kashechewan behind me. Chalk it up to an educational experience, an expensive life lesson on the history of the reserve system, the resilience of the Cree people, and my own emotional limits. But I could not. For starters Kashechewan was still in the news. The crises kept coming. There was the housing shortage at the end of 2011; the fuel crisis in the winter of 2012; the flooding problems in the springs of 2012, 2013, 2014, 2015, and 2016.

Reading these stories, I wondered how the crises were affecting those I had met on the reserve. Whether they would survive another winter. How many would go without food. How many would commit suicide.

The main theory used to explain these conditions is that they are the unfortunate remnant of policies that we now acknowledge as a historic mistake. As a national myth, so oft-repeated it has gained the familiarity of a nursery rhyme, it has the advantage that any wrongdoing is embedded firmly in the past. But evidence for a definitive shift in aims is noticeably lacking. For most of history, the goal has been to prepare "Indians" for life down south, i.e., to assimilate. It was the aim of many historic policies, including the residential schools and the Indian Act. Perhaps this is the quickest way to bring it about: letting the conditions on the reserves become so unlivable that anyone with the means would abandon them and move south. This viewpoint might seem callous, but it sheds some light on why there have been all those reports — the Provincial justice inquiries in Ontario (2007) and Manitoba (2001), Royal Commission on Aboriginal Peoples (1996), Penner Report (1983), and the Hawthorn Report (1967) — commissioned at great cost and, once completed, their recommendations promptly shelved.

As I began to recover, to gain distance and perspective, I returned to the stories that I had heard and tried to understand if and how they fit into the larger narrative. I began researching the history of Kashechewan and other reserves to find out the causes of the Third World conditions. To connect these threads together, I filed Access to Information and Privacy (ATIP) requests to discover what had really happened during Kashechewan's 2005 water crisis.

This is what I found out.

THIRTEEN

The Crisis

Remember this — we are people. [You] used to call us human beings.
— Kashechewan elder William Sutherland

On the morning of October 14, 2005, there was very little about the day to suggest that it was about to become a national crisis. It was a sleepy Friday. That time of the year is known as *niskiskou*, Cree for plenty of geese, when the birds nest and rest along the Albany. Several residents, including the water plant's supervisor, Alfred Wesley, were out in the bush catching a few birds for the winter.

At 1:35 p.m. that day, Health Canada sent Chief Leo Friday a fax that the water was contaminated with E. coli. It was a health concern, but alas, not totally unexpected. The water had been on boil water advisory for the past two years. Sometimes, the water ran clear as an arctic stream, and at others, it was the colour of mud. The plant suffered from the same issue that plagues many First Nations communities. Isaiah Wynne, who manned it officially but did not have a valid water operator's license, should not have been working there alone, says John Gentile. As a precaution, many already drank bottled water.

That probably would have been the end of it had it not been for the shadow of Walkerton. The water on 75 percent of reserves poses a medium to high risk to human health.[1] On average 4.6 boil water advisories are issued each day.

But the E. coli notice coupled with the memories of what had happened five years earlier in Walkerton, a sleepy southern Ontario town, spurred immediate action. In 2000, seven people had died and twenty-five hundred people had become ill because of bad water. It was a national crisis and should not be allowed to happen again.

On the same day the water tested positive for E. coli, Health Canada called Chris LeBlanc, the field manager at Northern Waterworks. He had a reputation for efficiency and thoroughness. Chartering a plane to Kashechewan, he arrived the next morning and immediately went to work. There were two issues: the water lacked chlorine, the result of a broken chlorine injector found in the nine-year-old treatment plant; and the coagulant chemical aluminum sulfate, which is used to remove discolouration, wasn't working with the water's cold temperatures. LeBlanc ordered another coagulating agent, polyaluminum chloride, from neighbouring Fort Albany and Attawapiskat, and it arrived later that day.

Meanwhile the band council, too, was gathering forces. Chief Friday had contacted Lloyd McDonald, the fifty-two-year-old principal of St. Andrew's elementary school. He was known to be a committed advocate for First Nations, having worked in other schools on northern reserves. On the afternoon of October 14, 2005, he closed the elementary school and the secondary school followed suit. Together, he and Chief Friday formed a core committee to manage the water crisis, which was comprised of Deputy Chief Rebecca Friday, Health Director Edward Sutherland, the crisis coordinator John Koosees, and several teachers, including Carol Laronde. "There were all sorts of discussions but the main one was how to get attention from Health Canada to step in and help," explained Mr. Sutherland. A press release was sent to the media. Kashechewan's water crisis was first picked up in the *Timmins Daily Press* on October 18, 2005. In an article on October 19, 2005, the *Canadian Press* said that Kashechewan residents had long been exposed to dirty water, which was causing "skin infections, gastrointestinal disorders, headaches and fevers." In an article that day in *Yahoo! News*, the contaminated water was said to cause "chronic diarrhea and scabies."

All of the confusion and accusations surrounding the water crisis had as much to do with timing as anything else. Since October 15, Mr. LeBlanc had been living inside Kashechewan's water plant. Tests for E. coli normally take about twenty-eight hours, and so by October 17th, according to Health Canada, the water was officially clear of this and other coliform bacteria. The water ran clear, according to LeBlanc, and chlorine levels were also below Ontario's standard recommended maximum of four milligrams per litre. And the plant was in better shape than it had been in years. Mr. LeBlanc told the chief and Kashechewan's executive director Archie Wesley of these results.

When I asked Elijah Wesley, former acting principal of St. Andrew's school, whether he knew the water was clean, he said he had heard that rumour from one of the nurses. But he had also heard the contrary, which was reportedly supported by a letter from an "environmental officer." With the weight of authority of the official document, he chose to believe the government representative, as did many other residents, when interviewed about the crisis five years later.

With the growing press coverage, the Ministry began to fly bottled water to the community. On October 19, 2005, it sent Indian Affairs Minister Andy Scott to the embattled First Nation. The arrival of Mr. Scott was a big coup for an impoverished community of 1,800. Most of the dealings between reserves and the Ministry involve long distance communication and delays. It is widely believed that this allows the department to have an arm's-length relationship, and to ignore the ongoing human rights crisis.

This wasn't the first time that the band council had tried to raise awareness of its social conditions and economic issues. It had gone to the Ministry with its overcrowding issues, the poor housing conditions, mould, and flooding. It had asked for help with unemployment, poverty, arson, and overpriced food. It had requested resources to deal with its suicide crisis and the legacy of the residential schools. Whenever it had asked for help, the Ministry had told the band council that it was not possible. The official reason was that it was a matter of money. Ottawa was unprepared to help while the "deficit was too large," explains former Kashechewan Chief Leo Friday. "They said that, if we wanted more money, we had to show them 'a financial recovery plan,' i.e., how we would become financially sustainable as a community. How we would repay them. But we couldn't do that because they turned down all our plans for employment schemes."

With Mr. Scott's trip, the community would be able to talk to the Minister directly about how they were trapped. But his arrival also created a problem. A federal minister was flying to town to examine the contaminated water. What was coming out of the taps was clean. Someone, although their identity remains unknown, came up with a solution: river water. Before Mr. Scott arrived, some in the community gathered it up in glasses, jars, and bottles, and placed them on the table where the Ministry officials were scheduled to be seated at that evening's gathering in the school gym.[2] During the meeting with Health Canada and INAC, Kashechewan's leadership, and the community, these props were used to great effect: to heighten the drama, several angry residents told the Canadian government officials, "You drink the water." No one did.

From the transcripts of that meeting, some in the community genuinely thought that the water was still polluted. A rumour had surfaced, which was subsequently reported in the media, that the water intake was located directly downstream from the raw sewage outflow. Although this later turned out to be false, according to documents released by INAC, what was true was the berm that diverted the water waste away from the uptake source had been breeched. If fecal matter was flowing towards the drinking water source, contamination could easily recur, and this was causing genuine anxiety in the community.

And for many, the issue had surpassed water and was symbolic of the delays that they had been forced for years to drink. One after another stood to speak in English or Cree. They demanded better schools, removal of the diesel-contaminated soil underneath their elementary school, which had spilled two years previously but the band didn't have the tools to clean up. They wanted more housing: there were up to eighteen people living per house, and children were sleeping in shifts. They demanded flooding protection beyond the failing dyke. They wanted better living conditions: the houses were rotting and mouldy, and children were getting sick. "A long time ago, my grandfathers had to leave their hunting grounds," explained Kashechewan elder William Sutherland. "They gave us a piece of land which is a swamp. My people are tired. My children are tired. My grandkids are tired. They are tired of being kicked around all the time. Remember this — we are people. [You] used to call us human beings."

Mr. Scott listened closely. When the room had quietened, he stood up. "I think that this situation has been neglected for too long and it needs to be fixed. And I want to work with your leadership to figure out the plan to do that. No more band-aid solutions."[3]

Everyone clapped. That night he left by plane. The community waited.

Over the next few days, there was no mention of any of these demands in the media coverage of the unfolding crisis. Rather than fixing the flooding issue, housing problem, contaminated soil, overpriced food, or unemployment, INAC promised to send in bottled water. It would deliver 43,200 litres to the community by the end of the week.

Worse, media interest in the story began to ebb. There had been an E. coli warning in a remote northern community, resulting in a boil water advisory. It was more common than not. There were 127 other First Nation communities also on boil water advisories,[4] and the story struggled to make it past A7 in the *Globe and Mail*. In the subsequent days, most newspapers stopped covering it.

As the media interest died down, the community brainstormed about what to do, according to Edward Sutherland. They decided to invite someone to the community who already had a reputation for going the extra mile to help First Nations communities: Dr. Murray Trusler, chief of staff at Weeneebayko General Hospital in Moose Factory, Ontario.

On October 21, 2005, Dr. Lindsay MacMillan was at home having a few Friday-night beers with friends in her Moose Factory apartment. At about 6:00 p.m., she received a call from her supervisor, Dr. Trusler. He wanted a favour, he explained. Had she heard about the water crisis in nearby Kashechewan? And was she prepared to accompany him to check it out?

The next morning, MacMillan, Trusler, and David Bowen flew in on a helicopter and began home visits, looking for symptoms of E. coli.

"The houses were so dirty and dilapidated," explains Dr. MacMillan, who is now a family doctor in Huntsville, Ontario. "I went to one of the homes, and there were about ten kids all under eight, cramped into a tiny home with writing on the walls. The toilet looked like that one in the movie *Trainspotting*. It was blocked up and there was crap everywhere. It was disgusting, but also really sad."

The doctors treated the immediate health problems on the reserve, including asthma, diabetes, heart disease, ringworm, scabies, and impetigo. Since the skin problems had been allowed to grow and fester until raw and scabby, they resembled the grotesque diseases found in nineteenth-century medical dictionaries. Photos of these conditions and information from the band council's press releases started to appear in the national newspapers from October 25, 2005, onwards, with headlines and captions that said, "Deadly E-coli threatens natives, 2,000 on reserve need vaccinations,"[5] and "Mary-Joe, 12, shows hand sores that have developed after washing in tainted tap water."[6]

Midway through, Dr. Trusler flew to Queen's Park to give media interviews that the community might be infected with Hepatitis A and B from the contaminated water. Vaccinations were urgently needed. Years later, members of Kashechewan's leadership still talked of him in glowing terms: he gave us "more support" (Edward Sutherland); "he flew in on a helicopter" (John Koosees, true); and "he paid for the trip himself" (John Koosees, although false).

With Dr. Trusler in Queen's Park, MacMillan and Bowen were left to finish the home visits. On her last day in Kashechewan, MacMillan was confronted by two Health Canada representatives who had flown into the community once Trusler's photographs hit the papers. The man and woman cornered her in a small meeting room. There, she was warned she had caused serious problems by violating protocol. "Health Canada's representatives completely bawled us out. They slapped our wrists and gave us a talking to and said, 'You haven't gone through the proper channels.' But by then, the pictures had already reached the *Globe and Mail*."

Today, there's more of an understanding among different First Nations about how public interest in human rights can be used to embarrass the federal government into action. For example, Attawapiskat First Nation's 2011 housing crisis became a platform to raise the larger issue: the crushing poverty was adjacent to hundreds of millions of dollars of diamonds being extracted at the Victor De Beers mine. In October 2013, Pukatawagan First Nation, nine hundred kilometres north of Winnipeg, capitalized on UN indigenous rights investigator James Anaya's visit to Canada to spotlight their crippling suicide rates, which are among the world's highest, higher than any other country in the world, and outranked only by other First Nations communities in Canada.

But in 2005, Kashechewan First Nation was one of the first to see the media's potential. On October 25th, in a meeting that would seal Kashechewan's fate, Dr. Trusler sat down with Premier Dalton McGuinty and David Ramsay, Ontario's natural resources and Aboriginal affairs minister. Dr. Trusler came prepared. He and others on the reserve had prepared a Power Point presentation. Questions like: "Are we going to continue to accept that when we bathe in the water that simple cuts can turn into this?" were placed adjacent to photos of scabrous, limb-long sores, and jugs of brown water. Also documented were close-ups of children's faces marred by advanced scabies, ringworm, and impetigo; yellow toenails blemished with a dark fungus; a blocked toilet smeared with excrement.

Ramsay called Trusler "a hero" for his work. Later that day, McGuinty decided to evacuate the town and declared Kash to be in a state of emergency.

Aboriginal issues divide along federal and provincial lines; on-reserve is Ottawa's jurisdiction and off-reserve is the province's. With different mandates, they have a reputation for lack of coordination on reserve policy. This time was no different. The Ministry ignored the ongoing evacuation and began to inundate the reserve with filtered water. Three hundred and fifty thousand litres of H_2O was to be shipped in Bombardier Dash 8s and Hercules planes. Another 140,000 litres would be produced *in situ* through DART. As a water emergency plan, it was excellent. Each person on the reserve would receive eighteen litres per day, delivered by the military, Kashechewan's police, and local volunteers. Filtered water would be provided around the clock for drinking, cooking, dish washing, and bathing. It began to accumulate. Many in the town had realized that the crisis was greatly exaggerated and were back to drinking their water straight from the tap. The DART's water bags could not be stacked and stored, for fear they would break. Eventually, they were laid out in rows in whatever public space was available, including the church basement, the nursing station, the high school, and the sports rink. Access to Information documents released the following year[7] revealed the military were frustrated by the whole operation. "Although an excellent PR exercise, the true need of the detachment was never established."

With the arrival of the military, the public outrage about the conditions on the reserve had reached a fever pitch. Kashechewan became a matter of national pride. With the television, radio, and newspaper coverage, hundreds of people began writing to the prime minister and the Ministry saying they were ashamed to be Canadian. "I am horrified and disgusted that the government has neglected these people to this extent. How many other reserves are subjected to similar treatment, I wonder. Why are we taking better care of people from other countries than we are of our own?" emailed a member of the public to Minister Scott on October 25, 2005. Another email from the same day presented him with a list of questions: "What have you done so far to improve our brothers and sisters right to a decent life rather than allow them to live in squalor? How much longer are you willing to wait for repairs to begin on the Kashechewan filtration plant? Why are you playing what appears to be Russian roulette with the health of the Kashechewan people? Are they not as important as their neighbours in the Southern part of Canada?" An email to the prime minister on October 28, 2005: "I can't believe it had to come to this.… I hope something is done soon. And not just taking them away … making a new reservation … and improving the living conditions, jobs and medical care."

Both levels of government — Ontario and Ottawa — were eager to sidestep the blame. There were several irate newspaper editorials criticizing the deplorable conditions on reserves across Canada. Kashechewan, like many First Nations, had gotten caught in the middle of jurisdictional wrangling, while its problems worsened and were largely ignored, according to the *Globe*. "The Premier is lucky to have the federal government as a foil because the story of Kashechewan is filled with spectacularly boneheaded moves by Ottawa."[8]

In its defence, the province said Kashechewan was outside its mandate. It wasn't Ontario's fault, as Ottawa has "been missing in action," Premier Dalton McGuinty told reporters. David Ramsay, the provincial minister responsible for Aboriginal Affairs, told Queen's Park "the community has never made any direct demand to the province, nor would they want to, because they know that the federal government has a treaty obligation to take care of that community, as they do of all First Nation communities across this province. The First Nations guard that very, very carefully and they don't want the province coming in on that."[9] But if Kashechewan hadn't wanted the province to get involved, why had they gone to the province time and time again? countered Howard Hampton, Ontario's NDP leader. They had approached the Ontario government six months, one year, and two years previously, each time claiming they needed urgent help. And given that Ottawa's negligence was well-known, it was the province's moral duty to act. "The fact is everybody knew the federal government would not help these people," said Charlie Angus, the New Democrat MP for the federal riding of Timmins-James Bay. "And so I feel I have to ask, where was the province of Ontario in the face of post-Walkerton?"

The media, including the CBC and the *Globe and Mail*, arrived in Kashechewan to cover the water crisis on October 27, 2005, flown in on an air charter paid for by the NDP. By this time, the water had been clean for eleven days. For the past nine days, it had met all provincial and federal standards. And in the public relations battle, the Ministry v. Kashechewan, the public had clearly sided with the impoverished reserve.

From the news reports that were published and aired over the following days, the crisis seemed to be progressing according to plan. But in the behind-the-scenes coverage, a number of events seemed off. In a video shot by the CBC, the camera crew drove to what was supposed to be a rally. Neat rows of protest signs attached with identical white plastic tags to the chain link fence, said things like, "We are not invisible"; "We need help now! Not later"; "It's Our <u>Right</u> to Get Medical Treatment"; and "We need clean water for our children. We need help now. We don't want our children to be infected with E. coli. Immediate evacuation." A group of locals examined them like art in a gallery, moving from sign to sign, pointing and smiling. Nearby a crowd of people chatted. Some were smoking, others waved to the camera; one child around the age of seven played with his slingshot. Supposedly a medical emergency, it had a festive feeling, like a public holiday.

Until then, Kash's water had been in the public eye for more than a week, always the colour of murky ginger ale. Eager to investigate, Global TV reporter Sean Mallen and crew visited a home where the windows were boarded up with plywood and "Outlawz" was graffitied onto the porch. Nineteen people lived in a three-bedroom home, and many were milling about in the kitchen.

A thirtysomething woman turned on the tap while the camera filmed. The water was clean and clear. "I'm drinking tap water!" another shouted, and the camera panned to a group of ladies standing near the sink and drinking the clear liquid from glasses. Mallen looked stressed. He turned to the woman.

"Do any of your kids have a really bad rash?"

"Just me," she replied.

"Where is it?" Pause. "In a place you can show me?"

Pulling up her shirt, she sucked in her stomach, which was filled with advanced ringworm. She giggled embarrassedly. Mullen leaned in confidentially, sensing her discomfort. "I'm really sorry," he said. "What happens when you put the water on the rash?"

No answer.

"Does it hurt?"

"Yeah!"

"Now do any of your children have any kind of rash?"

They both looked around the room. Silence. Another woman pointed at the little boy nearby suggesting he had head lice. Some smiled at the joke.

As it became increasingly apparent that the skin diseases that had appeared in Dr. Trusler's photos were not caused by E. coli, the story changed: the official reason the reserve needed to be evacuated was that Mr. LeBlanc had put too much chlorine in the water, although his records suggested otherwise.

By then, all levels of government were interested in containing the crisis. Prime Minister Paul Martin said the federal government would "open wide its cheque book," and do "whatever is necessary." Ottawa would spend an estimated 300 million dollars to rebuild at a new location on higher ground so Kashechewan would no longer flood. There would be jobs for locals in the relocation and rebuilding of the community.

Beyond its borders, there would be investment throughout the region. Technically, health care on reserves is supposed to be a federal responsibility. But with Ottawa's lousy reputation, the dearth is partly made up by a "patchwork of services" run by anyone who steps up to the plate: the province, municipalities, and band councils. Like the issue with the fire department or emergency flooding, the absence of a coordinated response or overarching plan means healthcare on reserves tends to lurch from one crisis to the next.

The water crisis pressured Ottawa into action. On October 27, 2005, Ottawa announced a plan to create a "First Nations Health Organization" in the area to better integrate this patchwork of services and "be more responsive to the unique health needs of this region."

Suicide too would receive long-overdue attention. The issue impacts many aspects of everyday life, from students who quit school when they lose someone close, the unresolvable sense of loss to the victim's friends and family, and the anxiety about the possibility of suicide clusters that paralyzes the community. The urgency of the tragedy is heightened only by its familiarity. To tackle the issue, Ottawa promised to "enhance family violence and suicide prevention services" throughout the area, and offer "counselling, psychological supports and youth outreach" to Kashechewan and others in the region.

Finally, water on reserves would become a priority. Ottawa would implement a $1.6 billion national strategy. According to this plan, in three years, it would achieve what had eluded every federal government since Ottawa had begun actively implementing social programs on the reserves in 1951. By 2008, the number of contaminated and at-risk water systems would be reduced from their current figure of three-quarters of all reserves to 16 percent.

The water crisis was extended beyond its lifespan, but it had delivered more than anyone could have imagined.

FOURTEEN

Where Next?

I'm an Indian. I haven't heard many promises I believed anyway.
— Spokane/Coeur d'Alene poet Sherman Alexie

While the reserve appeared to have every reason to celebrate, behind the scenes, many were cautious. The history of broken promises is as long as the historic record. It had been part of Kashechewan's story from its beginning, when people were forced onto a flood plain against their will, or when their children were kidnapped during the Sixties Scoop and they were lied to about what had happened. Beyond the reserve, this dynamic is familiar to any indigenous person, with many agreements ignored, whether the Two Row Wampum of 1613, Royal Proclamation of 1763, or the Numbered Treaties of the nineteenth century. As Harold Cardinal wrote, "only fools believe even the most righteous assurances from those who consistently have refused to honour previous commitments, and only fools go on accepting forever further promises from such people."[1]

The people of Kashechewan were determined not to be counted among those fools. To avoid the possibility of this historic amnesia, the First Nation used the evacuation as a bargaining chip, and in phone calls with various branches of government, they delayed their return. It was expensive to keep the First Nation in hotels. And embarrassing. As long as the Kashechewan First Nation were displaced, the story still had legs.

In late November, the Associated Press picked up the story, as did the Rome-based Inter Press Service.

This in itself was astonishing. A northern Ontario reserve of 1,800 had become a major news story with a water crisis that was partially staged. The international attention was key. Some of the biggest gains on First Nations rights have come from the embarrassment of outsiders looking in. Examples include the American servicemen posted to Canada during the Second World War who complained to their representatives about the conditions of Canadian reserves, which helped instigate the 1951 changes to the Indian Act; the delegation of First Nations leaders that went to London in 1980 to lobby for Aboriginal rights in the Constitution Act, which led to the addition of section 35; Chief Louis Stevenson inviting South African ambassador Glenn Babb to his Peguis reserve in 1987 to highlight the similarities between the plight of blacks under Apartheid and Natives on the reserves.

Kashechewan's delaying tactic worked for long enough — four weeks — to secure promises on many of the key issues that hindered the community: housing, flooding protection, school infrastructure, healthcare, family violence, and mental health.

But as a long-term strategy, it was unsustainable. The community had been scattered across the nation, evacuated to wherever would take them: hotels and private houses in Attawapiskat, Cochrane, Moosonee, Ottawa, Peterborough, Sudbury, Temagami, and Timmins. This marred organization and communication.

Beginning November 28, 2005, the Ministry circumvented the leadership, and began airlifting Kashechewan residents back to the reserve in groups of about thirty people. To finalize the exit, Ottawa solicited evacuee exit dates from each of the host cities; the final three — Cochrane, Sudbury, and Timmins — scheduled for December 15th. If the evacuees were not gone by then, they would be transported to stay in the Nav Canada Centre, a conference and hotel complex in Cornwall. A November 14th military briefing note obtained through ATIP requests foreshadowed Kashechewan's legacy when it listed several reasons for containing the crisis, including setting an example to other troubled First Nations communities who might realize that they too could embarrass the government into action. "The success of the Kashechewan band to drawing attention to their plight increases the likelihood that other Native communities will adopt a similar approach."

On the day that INAC began sending the evacuees back to Kashechewan, the history of Canada took an unexpected turn. For those who had been following the revelations of the Gomery Commission, the November 28th vote of non-confidence in Prime Minister Paul Martin's government had been more than a year in the making. It marked a new era in First Nation–Ottawa relations; one marked more by unilateralism than inclusivity and consensus-building among First Nations, for which Mr. Martin, in his short time as national leader, had become known.

With his victory, Prime Minister Stephen Harper hired Alan Pope, a Timmins-based lawyer, progressive conservative, and former Ontario cabinet minister to decide Kashechewan's fate. On June 6, 2006, he became Special Federal Representative, tasked with interviewing Kashechewan's people and devising solutions to the flooding issue and their many social problems. On November 9, 2006, in a story widely covered by both national and international media, he released a report. It ignored the previous policies and urged them to move to a spot near Timmins. The relocation would improve their "individual and economic opportunities." By moving closer to an urban centre, they could escape poverty. They could visit their homelands on holiday.

The federal government quietly praised the report. But for the community, it felt like the continuation of the historic narrative of assimilation. If poverty had been the overarching concern, why had the Ministry refused or ignored each attempt by the reserve to rise above it? Since 1986, Kashechewan had submitted many job creation proposals, including the area's first environmentally friendly fishery, salt evaporation ponds, moose farm, clay-mining project, chicken hatchery, pig farm, lumber yard, and greenhouse. They had petitioned INAC for a wind farm. A few people had opened mom-and-pop shops, although with the ever present threat of arson and flooding, it was hard for these to make a profit.

None of the reserve's employment plans had been approved. Nor had the infrastructure that would make life liveable: a fire department or flooding protection. Instead, what was given the go ahead was another relocation, like that which had put them in the flood plain in the first place. In a vote on March 2007, the majority said no.

To understand why any indigenous community would choose not to relocate to an urban area, consider the history. They have been stripped of almost everything that defines them as people: their language, culture, religion, and traditional economies. Somehow they have endured. Their continued belief in their own existence, a phenomenon that philosophy professor Jonathan Lear calls "radical hope,"[2] can be puzzling to an outsider. The academic literature discussing what has sustained this belief is limited, but several indigenous writers and leaders have stepped in to fill the gap. Some, such as Reuben, believe it is *bimboleytosowin*, the concept described earlier that combines self-reliance, self-belief, and a trust in themselves that they can survive anything.

Others point to the ethic of radical care, such that every person is responsible for their fellow man. Many of the community's characteristics embody this idea. For example, no matter how crowded the houses, no one goes homeless. No matter who dies, there are no orphans on a reserve, for the community is expected to raise the child. No matter how poor, expenses such as funerals and weddings are shared among the community. A person can only fall so far before their Cree sisters and brothers will cushion their descent.

Still others, such as broadcaster and author Wab Kinew, point to spiritual ceremonies such as the sweat lodge or sun dance, which have made a comeback in the last twenty years, and are designed to strengthen a person's resilience and connection to the land.

It is hard to predict which of these ideas and practices, if any, would survive a move.

After Pope's study was rejected, the government ignored the promises that were made immediately after the water crisis, and instead adopted what in indigenous circles is called "the Canadian alternative to action"; or rather, the continued study of Kashechewan's residents. A second survey was conducted in 2007 that found that they wanted to move away from the flood plain but keep within their traditional area. It wasn't the answer that the government wanted (too expensive), so the report was ignored. A third study was conducted by Dr. Emily Faries, a professor of indigenous studies at the University of Sudbury, who was hired by the First Nation to study other possible locations away from the current flood plain. A fourth in 2010, the Capital Planning Study, evaluated the costs of staying put versus moving. A fifth in 2014, the Far field study, did the same thing. That investigation is still ongoing at the time of writing.

Much of what has happened up to this time (with the exception of the staged water crisis) is familiar to anyone with a passing interest in First Nations issues. The people of Kashechewan had lost the majority of their land, been moved to a flood plain, and left there. Their children had been half starved, raped, and left to die in the residential schools. They had been kidnapped in the Sixties Scoop and the parents lied to. When they had tried to improve their situation, and overcome the toxic legacy of their past, all their attempts had been ignored.

This is the system that we have constructed. The legacy of that history is a very poor quality of life. The poverty is crippling. Children kill themselves. Occasionally, First Nations leaders become angry, but that dynamic has the uncomfortable familiarity of a cliché, and the sentiment is either pitied or ignored.

Sometimes, the community tries to garner public sympathy through the media. If the crisis is considered sufficiently sensational to be newsworthy, i.e., worse than all others, the reserve becomes national or even international news. Examples include the Mushuau Innu children sniffing gas in 1993, northern Ontario's Pikangikum for their suicide rates in 2000, Kashechewan for its water in 2005, Attawapiskat for its housing crisis in 2011 and its suicide epidemic in the spring of 2016. If the reserve is lucky, the outpouring of public sympathy might secure government funding and much-needed services.

But what if the reserve's situation is not actually worse than all others? Suppose the reserve has record-high suicide rates; undrinkable water the colour of sewage; mouldy houses where kids sleep in shifts; malnourished children, and extreme levels of sickness; but none of these issues has, as yet, caused any newsworthy deaths.

That was Kashechewan's situation in late 2005.

By all accounts it was worse than when I arrived five years later, when similar, albeit slightly improved conditions — crippling poverty, record-high suicide rates, traumatized and overwhelmed people — caused me to have PTSD.

The normalization of crisis ensures that only those reserves whose problems are so bad that they are emblematic of a larger failure gain the required help. We cherry-pick the most extreme cases to assuage our guilt and create the illusion that the situation is improving. The rest of the reserves are stuck in stasis. First Nations communities appear to be masters of their own destiny, but this chimera of autonomy masks the real situation whereby the Ministry runs reserves as they see fit.

We have become so used to this situation, so accustomed to the accompanying dependency, that when an alternative is proposed, it is labelled as unprecedented and an "experiment." Anything but a ward-state dynamic is predicted to somehow ruin the country.

"Many aboriginals believe deeply in the [sovereignty] model, as do their non-aboriginal supporters and increasingly the courts," wrote *Globe and Mail* columnist Jeffrey Simpson in the July 30, 2014, edition of the newspaper. "The model hasn't been tried, or worked, anywhere else."[3]

This widely held opinion is inaccurate. Native sovereignty is already a reality for several developed nations with indigenous populations. In New Zealand, indigenous sovereignty has existed for the past 176 years, since the 1840 treaty of Waitangi, the document on which the country is founded. It gives the Māori significant resource rights over the forests, fisheries, and their lands. Today, the Māori own about 37 percent of the nation's fisheries under the 1992 Sealord deal. They own 36 percent of the forests and 5.5 percent of the nation's land.

In the United States, Native sovereignty has been part of the nation for much of its history. In 1832, Chief Justice of the United States John James Marshall wrote his historic opinion in Worcester v. Georgia, which decreed that Native American tribes were "domestic dependent nations." In his Cherokee opinions of the early 1830s, he ruled that they were "nations like any other" requiring a government-to-government relationship.

To ensure that Native American tribes could function like nations, they were given several ways of generating income. They can tax their own citizens. They can form corporations that do not pay sales taxes. They can produce and sell cigarettes. They can set up casinos and other types of gaming on their land. They can sell the rights to all oil and gas deposits found on "Indian trust land," or process these resources themselves. They can invite investors to their land and set the conditions for any subsequent construction and development. They have the unfettered right to fish and hunt on reservation land, and to create commercial fisheries — in select sites off-reservation, subject to conservation efforts. For example, Milwaukee's Potawatomi Bingo Casino is the county's largest employer and the largest Indian casino in the world. It has four million visitors annually and revenues of $463 million ($360 million US) per year.

With this money, the Native American tribes have gained sovereignty over many areas of reserve life. They control their own courts, police, and child welfare service, as well as the economic development on reserves.

It is difficult to measure the differences in well-being between the two systems. But all the data we have, including the many studies published by the Harvard Project on American Indian Economic Development, point to Native sovereignty improving general quality of life. Our reserves are poorer than their counterparts south of the border. Our indigenous populations earn less than half — or 42 percent — of the national average. Though not without its problems, the US system scores significantly better on other indicators too, including unemployment, income, and suicide rates.

Changing the power dynamic will not happen overnight. Nor will it be a matter of just one policy or law. The situation has taken more than a century to create and it will take time to undo. At the time of writing, there had been several steps in the right direction, with the announcement of the inquiry into the murdered and missing indigenous women and girls, and the promise of the implementation of all of the Truth and Reconciliation Commission's 94 recommendations. However, there still needs to be a considerable injection of funds into the education system and a serious transfer of property rights and responsibilities to indigenous persons if we are to start to address and acknowledge our historic legacy and give people a fair shot in life.

If not, another generation of young people will grow up in conditions where their families run out of food each month, in mouldy homes that lack clean water, where yearly flooding causes months of panic, where kids fake their suicides so they can spend a few days in a safe place, where kids see death as the easiest option.

I could not survive in these conditions. No one else should have to.

Getting Involved

Reconciliation with Native People is still the most pressing social justice issue Canada faces.

That quote from author and Ojibway journalist Wab Kinew speaks to many aspects of reserve life, from the legacy of the residential schools and the Sixties Scoop, to the chronic underfunding of the schools and health care, to the top-down funding and power dynamic that exists on the reserves. Reconciliation is a matter of politicians and indigenous leaders coming together to form new policies and laws, but it also includes adjusting the dynamic of our daily lives. If you want to become involved, here are a few ways that you can help:

Help Kashechewan youth rediscover their traditions: The extermination of indigenous cultures, religions, and languages was the aim of several government policies including the residential schools, Potlatch laws, and the Indian Act. As a result many of Kashechewan's children are unaware of the Seven Sacred Teachings, the Red Road, and *bimboleytosowin*. Some kids interviewed have never left the bounds of their reserve except for medical care. Paddling with the Cree was started in the summer of 2016 to address these issues. Each summer, a group will undertake a major canoe trip, with cultural activities and spiritual teachings along the way. On the first trip, eighteen youth and six adults paddled for ten days from Hearst,

Ontario, to Kashechewan, a distance of approximately four hundred kilometres. You can find out more and ensure that the program continues by donating at www.rotaryhip.com.

Work towards better indigenous health: First Nations health care is chronically underfunded compared to the rest of Canada, and that combined with the social conditions, means higher rates of several diseases. For example, the rates of HIV on reserves are ten times higher than in the rest of the country. On average, the incidence of tuberculosis is thirty-four times higher. The Ottawa-based charity First Nations Child and Family Caring Society of Canada runs a program called *Many Hands, One Dream*. It is a long-term initiative to foster collaboration, and develop and implement solutions that will improve the health of Aboriginal children in Canada. See https://fncaringsociety.com.

Advocate for better food security: Canada's reserves have higher rates of food insecurity than other developed nations with indigenous populations, namely United States and Greenland. In Kashechewan and in many northern reserves, many families run out of food each month. The Assembly of First Nations (www.afn.ca) supports research into food security and advocates on behalf of First Nations.

Abolish the Indian Act: The Indian Act profoundly affects every aspect of life on reserves. It makes it impossible for First Nations to own their own land or build wealth, and highly limits the creation of jobs and economic investment. Please consider supporting political reform by writing to your local MP.

Help youth in education: In Kash and many impoverished reserves, 70 percent of students drop out of high school. On average, 58 percent of First Nations teenagers leave high school before graduation, according to information from 2011 National Household Survey. The issue impacts all aspects of community life, including the power dynamic between locals and outsiders, lack of wealth creation, and the negotiation and impact of the Impact Benefit Agreements between mining companies and First Nations. Indspire is an indigenous-led charity that aims to close this gap by offering scholarships to students and mentorship programs, and delivering programs to reserve schools. You can find out more at indspire.ca. Also, the Martin Aboriginal Education Initiative focuses on delivering programs that improve reading and writing skills for Aboriginal students across Canada. Check out www.maei-ieam.ca.

Target youth suicide: The suicide rate for First Nations reserves is five to seven times higher than the national average. Northern Ontario's rates are higher than anywhere else in the world, and are rising, according to a 2015 study published in the *Canadian Medical Association Journal*. The Toronto-based charity Canadian Roots Exchange organizes Native youth leadership programs and exchanges between indigenous and non-Aboriginal youth to promote mutual respect and understanding. See http://canadianroots.ca. The Ottawa-based Legacy of Hope Foundation is devoted to raising awareness of the legacy of residential schools and helping families and their survivors heal. See www.legacyofhope.ca.

Support Native artists: There are many talented First Nations writers, visual artists, musicians, filmmakers, dancers, drummers, and historians that rely on your interest and support. Their stories are vital to understanding the ongoing narrative of the country. First Nations publishers include Theytus (Penticton, BC), Kegedonce Press (Cape Croker First Nation, Wiarton, ON), Gabriel Dumont Institute Publishing (Saskatoon, SK), Ningwakwe Learning Press (Saugeen First Nation, Southampton, ON), Pemmican Publications Inc. (Winnipeg, MB), and Saskatchewan Indian Cultural Centre (Saskatoon, SK). The Bay of Spirits gallery sells and displays indigenous art. See www.bayofspirits.com.

Timeline of the 2005 E. coli Water Crisis

October 12	·	Water tested by Health Canada.
October 14	·	E. coli found in the water by Health Canada.
	·	Kashechewan band office warned about E. coli in the water.
	·	Elementary and high schools close in the afternoon.
October 15	·	Water engineer Chris LeBlanc is sent by Health Canada to the community. He fixes the broken water chlorine injector, which takes four hours, then adds the correct amount of chlorine to the water. The coagulant poly-aluminum chloride is also flown in from Fort Albany and Attawapiskat so that the filters can remove the particulate matter which causes the water discolouration.
October 17	·	Water found negative for E. coli and other bacteria according to Health Canada tests.
	·	Water runs clear according to Mr. LeBlanc.
October 18	·	E. coli story breaks in the *Timmins Daily Press*.
October 19	·	INAC Minister Andy Scott and other government officials arrive in Kashechewan. The officials are given brown river water to drink.
	·	Federal government announces it will fly bottled water onto the reserve.
	·	First mention of the story in the national media.

October 20	·	Leo Friday urges an evacuation until a new filtration system is in place.
	·	First mention of E. coli contaminated water in the *Globe and Mail*.
October 22	·	Dr. Murray Trusler, Dr. Lindsay MacMillan, and David Bowen fly to the community. Touring the reserve, they see and treat seventy-two people within three days, who are suffering from skin conditions and other health problems. They take photos of the patients and the overcrowded conditions, which are sent to the media. Dr. Trusler leaves two days later.
	·	Band council issues press releases calling for an immediate evacuation.
October 24	·	Bottled water starts to arrive in the community.
October 25	·	Premier Dalton McGuinty and Ontario Minister of Indian Affairs David Ramsay meet with community leaders and Dr. Trusler at Queen's Park.
	·	Announcement that Ontario government will evacuate 60 percent of the reserve's population. Ontario declares a state of emergency.
October 26	·	Ontario Emergency Management arrives in Kashechewan and starts the evacuation of 1,100 people.
	·	Prime Minister Paul Martin criticized for "systematic negligence" and "tragedy" at the reserve.
	·	A *Toronto Star* journalist travels to Kashechewan and publishes the first story from inside the community.
October 27	·	Federal government agrees with Kashechewan leadership and other First Nations leaders to move the community to higher ground.
	·	A *National Post* reporter flies to Kashechewan and publishes the paper's first story on location.
October 29	·	*Globe and Mail* declares Kashechewan a "national tragedy."
October 30	·	The Disaster Assistance Response Team (DART) and military rangers arrive in Kashechewan with portable water purification equipment and start producing clean water.

Notes

Introduction

1. In 1868, chief of Kanesatake, Joseph Onasakenrat, petitioned Ottawa
    to return the land around Oka to the Mohawks (as per the historical
    agreement) and was ignored, however, his successors would continue
    the fight across generations. The following century, the disagreement
    would reach boiling point with the 1990 Oka Crisis. In 1919, Freder-
    ick Ogilvie Loft, a Mohawk from the Six Nations of the Grand River
    Reserve, began the first pan-indigenous organization, the League of
    Indians of Canada, to change living conditions on the reserves. The
    government responded by ignoring all his communications, and
    declaring him a radical and dangerous, so Loft wrote articles about
    the cause for the *Globe* and *Saturday Night*, and travelled for years
    to raise awareness, eventually falling ill and dying, perhaps due to
    overwork. Bernard Ominayak was chief of the Lubicon Lake Cree
    from the late 1980s onwards, and for years, he fought for his people's
    inclusion in Treaty 8, however he was largely dismissed by the pro-
    vincial and federal governments until a road block on October 19,
    1988 that drew national and international attention, including from
    the U.N. Afterwards, the government hashed out an agreement.
2. As of December 31, 2014, 91 First Nations communities across Can-
    ada were on boil water advisory.

3. Staff, "Uprooted Aboriginals in Ontario await aid," Associated Press, November 13, 2005.
4. Staff, "Finanzspritze für Indianerreservation," ("Cash injection needed for Indian Reservation,") *Die Presse*, August 24, 2007.
5. Real Property Consulting Group, "First Nations Police Services: Building Condition Report & Needs Analysis for N.A.P.S. Detachments in Northern Ontario." Prepared for Solicitor General of Canada, August 20, 2001.
6. Pamela Matthews, "Detachment lacked infrastructure: Luloff," *Wawatay News*, April 30, 2009.

1: Moving North

1. The Ministry is the Orwellian sounding name for the Aboriginal Affairs and Northern Development Canada (AANDC) in the Indian Act, which is the list of laws that govern reserve life. Previous titles include The Indian branch, Indian Department, the Office of the Deputy Superintendent General of Indian Affairs, Department of Indian Affairs, Department of Indian and Northern Development, Indian and Northern Affairs Canada, or the current, AANDC. To avoid confusion, I have used the terms "The Ministry" or "the department" throughout this book's text.

2. Like many of the laws governing the reserves, this one was created in the late nineteenth century. Segregation was considered best for Aboriginals as it was then widely believed they were too "simple" to cope with extended contact with whites. In order to "civilize" them in a timely manner, only persons committed to the government's assimilationist agenda were allowed onto reserves, i.e. priests and nuns, Hudson's Bay managers, and Indian Agents, a system of social control that perversely allowed the widespread abuse in residential schools to continue unchecked. Isolation was further implemented by criminalizing people's free movement between the reserves, and by banning outsiders from visiting, laws both amended in 1985. According to Upper Canada Lieutenant-Governor Sir Francis Bond Head, whose writing and ideas shaped much of the current Indian

Act, "The greatest Kindness that we can perform towards these intelligent, simple-minded people is to remove and fortify them as much as possible from all Communication with the Whites."

3. This name has been changed at the doctor's request. Many people interviewed were anxious about offending the band council or the Ministry, and potentially affecting future funding. See Chapter 5 for more details.

2: The Fourth World

1. See J. Bonta, "Native Inmates: Institutional Response, Risk and Needs," *Canadian Journal of Criminology*, 31, no. 1 (1989): 49-62; F. Gale, *Aboriginal Youth and the Criminal Justice System: The Injustice of Justice?* (Cambridge: Cambridge University Press, 1990); Monture-Angus, P.A., "Lessons in Decolonization: Aboriginal Over-representation in Canadian Criminal Justice System," in *Visions of the Heart: Canadian Aboriginal Issues* (Toronto: Harcourt Canada, 2000), 361–86.

2. Other examples include Neil Stonechild, who died of hypothermia on the outskirts of Saskatoon in 1990, shortly after being in police custody. Known as a "starlight tour," this practice of taking First Nations people to the edge of town in the dead of winter and abandoning them is also alleged to have happened in 2000 to Darrel Night, Rodney Naistus, and Lawrence Wegner. In 2003, Saskatoon police chief Russell Sabo admitted there was a possibility it had been happening for years, after revealing that in 1976 an officer was disciplined for driving an Aboriginal woman to the edge of town and leaving her there.

3. Neither Statistics Canada nor the Ministry had any figures on Kashechewan's average salary, nor the average amount given to the population in benefits. This figure was calculated by averaging the mean salary for the reserve for those who work ($23,000), and the average monthly welfare, which was calculated by interviewing Kashechewan's unemployed population and averaging the amount given by Ontario Works ($383 per month), the National Child Benefit, and Ontario Family Benefit.

4. All the figures at PPP from 2014 International Monetary Fund.
5. The Expert Panel on the State of Knowledge of Food Security in Northern Canada, "Security in Northern Canada: An Assessment of the State of Knowledge," Council of Canadian Academies, 2014.
6. G.M. Egeland, "International Polar Year Inuit Health Survey: Health in Transition and Resiliency," Centre for Indigenous Peoples' Nutrition and Environment, McGill University, May 2010.

3: Meeting the Chief

1. This was according to John Gentile.
2. We don't know how many people were banished from their communities. The Indian Agent had multiple roles, acting as prosecutor, defence, judge, and jury for these decisions and he was not obligated to keep any records. He could banish people for breaking the many laws of the Indian Act or "seditious activity," i.e., failing to obey his commands. There are many anecdotal records of this happening; see Katherine Pettipas, *Severing the Ties that Bind: Government Repression of Indigenous Religious Ceremonies on the Prairies* (Winnipeg: University of Manitoba Press, 1994). Scholars estimate hundreds were arrested.
3. In 1967, two students Joel Wesley, his friend, Abraham Nakogee, both sixteen, were told to do some extra laps around the school's track after exercise class had ended and the rest of the students had left for the day. After a few laps, Nakogee complained of chest pains to the gym instructor, Brother Lauzon. He was told to stop whining and to keep going because he was fat. He complained again. The teacher ignored him. After a few more laps, he laid down on the track. A few minutes later, he died of a heart attack. Joel had witnessed what had happened. He was told to remain silent or he would face severe punishment, which in a place with severe beatings and an electric chair, was a terrifying warning. For more details, see Edmund Metatawabin, with Alexandra Shimo, *Up Ghost River: A Chief's Journey Through the Turbulent Waters of Native History* (Toronto: Knopf, 2014).
4. Laurie Gough, "All the lost boys and girls," *National Post*, November 19, 2005.

5. After six years contacting potential plaintiffs from reserves across the province, this class action lawsuit, Brown v. Attorney General of Canada, representing 16,000 children is due to be tried at the Ontario Superior Court of Justice starting September 2016.

6. The language used in the Indian Act is obtuse and confusing at best. Legal scholars offer different interpretations on legalities, correct practices, and procedures. As it can be helpful to return to the source material, here are the sections in question:

INDIAN ACT, SECTION 35

Lands Taken for Public Purposes

Taking of lands by local authorities

"Where by an Act of Parliament or a provincial legislature Her Majesty in right of a province, a municipal or local authority or a corporation is empowered to take or to use lands or any interest therein without the consent of the owner, the power may, with the consent of the Governor in Council and subject to any terms that may be prescribed by the Governor in Council, be exercised in relation to lands in a reserve or any interest therein."

Procedure

Unless the Governor in Council otherwise directs, all matters relating to compulsory taking or using of lands in a reserve under subsection (1) are governed by the statute by which the powers are conferred.

Marginal note: Grant in lieu of compulsory taking

Whenever the Governor in Council has consented to the exercise by a province, a municipal or local authority or a corporation of the powers referred to in subsection (1), the Governor in Council may, in lieu of the province, authority or corporation taking or using the lands without the consent of the owner, authorize a transfer or grant of the lands to the province, authority or corporation, subject to any terms that may be prescribed by the Governor in Council.

INDIAN ACT, SECTION 53

Management of Reserves and Surrendered and Designated Lands

Transactions re surrendered and designated land

(1) The Minister or a person appointed by the Minister for the purpose may, in accordance with this Act and the terms of the absolute surrender or designation, as the case may be,

(a) manage or sell absolutely surrendered lands; or

(b) manage, lease or carry out any other transaction affecting designated lands.

7. Chinta Puxley, "Children die as Manitoba reserves struggle with inadequate firefighting," Canadian Press, October 30, 2014.

8. Information from 2010 Statistics Canada, median total income by Aboriginal identity, population aged 25–54.

9. "The department's interpretation had, as a consequence, that Aboriginals who wanted to lease land were not treated like adults, they were second-guessed or given protection like children are given," said Philippe Dufrense, director of litigation for the Human Rights Commission. Quoted in Jorge Barrera, "Tribunal: Strahl, department treated FNs entrepreneurs like 'children,'" accessed February 16, 2011, www.aptn.ca.

10. As before, this law embodies the nineteenth century values of the time written, when wealth was considered detrimental to First Nations people as it would morally corrupt their characters and "simple" lifestyles.

4: A Lead at the Garbage Dump

1. The Indian Act's anti-trade laws would be struck down in December 2014, although the other laws that limit growth and profit remain.

2. Staff, "Indian Act Inhibits Business Mohawks Tell Royal Commission," *Windspeaker* 11, no. 5 (1993).

3. "The attempt to combine a system of pupilage with the settlement of these people in civilized parts of the country, leads only to the embarrassment of the Government, expect of the Crown, a waste of resources of the province, and injury to the Indians themselves. The Indian loses all the good qualities of his wild state, and acquires nothing but the bias of civilization. He does not become a good settler, he does not become an agriculturalist or a mechanic. He

does become a drunkard and a debaucher." This statement is by Lord Sydenham in July 22, 1841, as quoted in the House of Commons Debates.

4. Shawn McCarthy, "Resource revenues could lift some First Nations out of poverty report urges," *Globe and Mail*, March 3, 2015.

5. Editor, "Ontario's Far North Act: Aboriginal Poverty or Prosperity?" *Canadian Mining Journal*, October 31, 2011.

6. From the Moose Cree First Nation Impact Benefit Agreement, signed September 17, 2007. The IBAs for Kashechewan and Fort Albany were modeled on that signed by the Moose Cree First Nation. "The [First Nation] band members shall have first priority for employment for any project-related activities within [First Nation] Homeland. [The First Nation] has established a Human Resources Inventory and recommends anyone interested in employment to register. DBC [DeBeers Canada] commits to having [First Nation] members in skilled, administrative, professional, scientific and management positions whenever persons demonstrate the competence and qualifications."

7. The Indian Act, see section 53 (see Chapter 3's note 6) and 57.
INDIAN ACT, SECTION 57
The Governor in Council (i.e. government of the day) may make regulations: providing for the disposition of surrendered mines and minerals underlying lands in a reserve.

8. Éric Dewailly and Evert Nieboer, "Exposure and Preliminary Health Assessments of the Oujé-Bougomou Cree Population to Mine Tailing Residues," Institut Montreal: National de Santé Publique du Québec, 2005.

9. Will Nicholls and Lyle Stewart, "Poisoned: Quebec Studies Confirm Fears that Waters near O-J Are Heavily Contaminated by Mine Tailings," *Nation*, August 19, 2005.

10. The Nisga'a Lisims government can make laws regarding their land, assets, citizenship, language, and culture. They received $196.1 million (in 1999 currency) more than 2,000 square kilometres of land, an annual allocation of salmon, entitlements to harvest other fish, moose, and other wildlife, and funding to deliver health, education, and social services to their people and others in the area.

11. The Seven Sacred Teachings are a guide to ethical living encompassing both practical advice and body of principles. To be a good person, the Teachings demand that one must learn how to live a life that respects all of creation. Before knowledge comes understanding, and mortality begins with observation of the surrounds. One learns how each species in the animal kingdom interacts, eats, hunts, plays, and lives in harmony with the rest of the environment. Each animal embodies a virtue, a way of being that can instruct daily life. The wolf's moral quality is humility, which it manifests by walking with its head down and living for the pack. Other animals that embody the sacred lessons are the bear (courage), eagle (love), beaver (wisdom), raven (honesty), buffalo (respect), turtle (truth). The Seven Sacred Teachings are common to many First Nations peoples, although the animals differ depending on the geographic region.

5: Welfare

1. These figures are pretty typical of the time. All Treaties (1-11) were modeled on the Robinson Treaty of 1850, which introduced the idea of total surrender of traditional land in exchange for some money. The Treaties also specified that each First Nation would be given a small plot of land to occupy (the reserves) and that they could hunt and fish over any remaining unsettled land.
2. From the July 11, 1905 diary of Indian Affairs employee Samuel Stewart.
3. Books that cover the Treaty-making process include Thomas Berger, *Northern Frontier, Northern Homeland: The Report of the Mackenzie Valley Pipeline Inquiry* (Ottawa: Minister of Supply and Services Canada, 1977); Heather Robertson, *Reservations Are for Indians* (Toronto: J. Lorimer, 1991); and John Long, *Treaty No. 9* (Montreal: McGill-Queen's University Press, 2010). All explore the deliberate ambiguities and false promises that enabled the indigenous dispossession that occurred with the signing of the Numbered Treaties. There were cryptic promises "to do something for you," or that the Queen "would like to take you by the hand."
4. See CP, H. of C. Debates, 3 sess., 3 Parl., 1876, p.752: Laws Respecting Indians, March 21, 1876.

5. *Journals of the Legislative Assembly of Upper Canada*, 1844–45. App. EEE.
6. In 1875, 1,500 Dakota migrated to Canada after fleeing the war of 1862 between the Dakota and the white settlers of Minnesota. Settling five miles north of the town of Griswold, Manitoba, they began cultivating the land in the summer of 1877, investing in the latest farm machinery and seeds, and producing abundant crops of wheat, turnips, potatoes, and carrots. With profits growing, they expanded beyond farm work to the sale of ponies, fish, skins, beadwork, baskets, rush mats, and wild fruits. Their problems began when they started to hire the local white workers. After complaints about unfair competition, the Indian Agents crushed their profitability by banning the purchase of farm equipment and taking over the marketing and sale of their produce. The Dakota complained and in response, the Ministry selected it's own man, Chief Tunkan Cekiyana, to run (and ruin) the First Nation, who was believed to be more accommodating to the Ministry's wishes. Many Dakota were incensed, and began to voice their objections around a spiritual leader named Wanduta. In January 1903, the Ministry travelled to Oak River, arrested him and brought him to Griswold, Manitoba to be tried. He was sentenced to four months of hard labour at Brandon Jail.
7. Writing in the *University Magazine* in 1913. Quoted in Katherine Pettipas, *Severing the Ties that Bind: Government Repression of Indigenous Religious Ceremonies on the Prairies* (Winnipeg: University of Manitoba Press, 1994).

6: Rumours

1. This point is difficult to detail fully in a footnote and would require a whole book to explore comprehensively, which I hope a Cree linguist will one day write. To provide an example, family relations are one of the grammatical suffixes that give inflected Cree nouns their meaning. A simple noun like "mother" has a "possessive prefix" that describes kinship ties. "My mother" (*nikâwiy*) is a slightly different word to "your mother" (*kikâwiy*), and words take on different associations and emotional power depending on the intensity of

the relationship. According to Reuben, the Cree language teaches us that we are social animals and, as the meaning of words comes from the bonds of community, "speaking Cree reminds us that we are never truly alone."

2. Any homophobia is most likely a cultural import from the residential schools. Traditionally, the Cree believed the Great Creator created some people from a different mould. They were known as *kama-tawatehsit* or the "special ones," i.e., queer or gay (twin-spirited). The "special ones" were not ostracized, they were simply accepted and integrated into daily life.

3. Taylor Clark, "The 8 ½ Laws of Rumor Spread," *Psychology Today*, November 1, 2008.

4. From 1942 to 1952, government-sponsored doctors such as Percy Moore and Indian Affairs branch superintendent of Medical Services and Canada's leading nutrition expert Dr. Frederick Tisdall conducted several experiments on children and adults in northern Ontario Aboriginal communities, without securing their permission, including deprived them of certain foods to discover the long-term effects of malnutrition.

7: Teaching the Children

1. Statistic from Nishnawbe-Aski Police annual report 2010–2011.

2. Kashechewan isn't an isolated case; there have been many reports on the issue. Almost every year, there's another one. In 2010, the Canadian Mortgage and Housing Corporation published a study that found that insurance companies didn't want to sell Aboriginal people property insurance because without fire departments on reserves, it was too risky. That same year, a federal study found that the fire death rate was ten times higher on reserves than in the rest of Canada. In 2013, the Fall Report of the Auditor General of Canada reported that Ottawa was not doing enough to manage emergencies such as flooding and fires. In 2015, judge Tracey Lord, investigating a fire on a Northern Manitoba reserve that killed three children and a grandfather, repeated that sentiment and encouraged

the implementation of 911 services for all reserves. Currently, the necessary services are marred by lack of money. That was the conclusion of Michael Ferguson, the Auditor General of Canada in his 2013 Fall Report. "The Department knows that the program's annual budget of about $19 million is not sufficient." Another issue is the lack of monitoring. There are no national fire safety standards on reserves. There are no federal or provincial policies on how many firefighters, hoses, or trucks are required for persons living on a reserve to be adequately safe. National criteria would create a benchmark against which to measure success or failure. And when they weren't met, there would be a yardstick to evaluate the problem, which could draw attention to it, according to a May 2010 memo to the Ottawa on the issue, from Brock Holowachuk, the emergency coordinator for the Manitoba regional office of Aboriginal Affairs and Northern Development Canada. In Holowachuk's words, "We might struggle ... with what will happen if standards are not met."

3. The Red Road embodies all the teachings, practices, ideas, and rituals that teach indigenous men and women how to be a valuable member of society, and lead a good life. It encompasses both principles, such as the Seven Sacred Teachings and *bimboleytosowin*, and the practices and rituals that instill those ideas such as the vision quests, shaking tent, sweat lodges, and the powwow.

4. In today's history books, when First Nations appear at all, they are usually mentioned as an addendum, often with half-formed explanations as to why they aren't in the main body of text. For example, Desmond Morton in *A Short History of Canada* has a five-page chapter titled First Nations, from a 395-page book. "Whatever their form of life, Native North Americans saw themselves as part of nature and not its masters. Though they fought other bands and nations, they had very little sense of territorial ownership." In other words, First Nations liked to fight. Not about anything in particular, and certainly not over land. They didn't need the land, because they had no sense of ownership. Which might be politically convenient, but is contrary to many historic documents, such as the Two Row Wampum Treaty or the Royal Proclamation of 1793. Other stories have been similarly sanitized. Here's what happened to the Beothuks (Bay-oh-thucks),

a Native group who used to live on the east coast of Newfoundland, according to Robert Bothwell's *The Penguin History of Canada*: "And despite efforts by the government to establish friendly contact, with an eye to preserving the race, the last known member of the tribe died in 1829." Unlike Morton's account, there are no obvious errors in this version of history. But what's left out changes the story significantly. As Bothwell writes, early meetings between the English, French, and the Beothuks were peaceful. However, in the summer of 1613, missionaries mistook the celebrations of the Aboriginal greeting party for aggression. They shot at them. Over the next century, the hostilities increased, mainly because the Beothuks, incensed that the trade promises had been broken and that the newcomers were taking over their land, began to steal from the settlers. As the aggression mounted, the French put a bounty on the heads of Beothuks. All sides — the English, French, and Mikmak — began killing them for money. There are accounts of men notching the butts of their guns according to the numbers of Natives killed. Newfoundlander and trapper Rodgers claimed to have killed sixty Beothuks by 1817. Trapper Noel Boss killed ninety-nine men, women, and children. By 1800, the settlers who called themselves Indian Killers had been a little too successful. There were only a handful of Beothuks left. Some had been scalped, some died by disease, others in slavery. Eager to "preserve the race," the British began cracking down on the sport hunting of Indians. It was believed by London that the only way to continue the race would be to capture a Beothuk, feed him, and explain to him in the nicest way possible that all appearances to the contrary, the hostilities had ceased. Fifty pounds was the reward for a living person. The bounty merely exacerbated their killing. The last Beothuk was reportedly killed in 1829. See Pierre Berton, *My Country* (Toronto: Penguin, 1976), 165; Robert Bothwell, *The Penguin History of Canada* (Toronto: Penguin Canada, 2006), 96; Harold Horwood, "The People Who Were Murdered for Fun," *Macleans Magazine*, October 10, 1959; Desmond Morton, *A Short History of Canada* (Toronto: McClelland & Stewart, 2001), 14.

5.   The Indian Act has been compared to South Africa's Apartheid legislation. While not identical in scope, several of the laws have similar

functions. In both countries, there was a special department to manage the Natives (Canada: the Department of Indian Affairs; South Africa: the Coloured Affairs Department); laws that discouraged mixed race marriages (Canada: Indian Act; South Africa's Prohibition of Mixed Marriages Act); laws limiting land ownership (Canada's Indian Act; South Africa's Native Trust and Land Act); laws creating a separate education system (Canada's Indian Act; South Africa's Bantu Education Act); laws banning or highly restricting voting (Canada: The Election Act, federal and provincial; South Africa's Representation of Natives Act); and laws legitimizing the forced relocations of blacks and Aboriginals (Canada's Indian Act; South Africa's Native Administration Act). South African officials visited Canada several times in the early and mid-twentieth century to examine and learn from the Canadian reserve system, the latest being in 1962 when the South African ambassador visited reserves in the west of the country telling officials he wanted to see how they were maintained and run.

8: The Double Standard

1. Geoffrey York, *The Dispossessed: Life and Death in Native Canada* (Toronto: Little Brown, 1992), 86.
2. M. Optis, K. Shaw, P. Stephenson, and P. Wild, "Mold Growth in On-reserve Homes in Canada: The Need for Research, Education, Policy, and Funding," *Journal of Environmental Health*, 2012.
3. "Diabetes in Canada: Facts and Figures from a Public Health Perspective," Public Health Agency of Canada, December 15, 2011.
4. "Obesity in Canada," Joint report by the Public Health Agency of Canada (PHAC) and Canadian Institute for Health Information (CIHI), June 20, 2011.
5. Staff, "Early infant mortality in Canada called 2nd worst in developed world," Canadian Press, May 8, 2013.
6. Julien Gignac, "Northern Ontario First Nations declare public-health emergency," *Globe and Mail*, February 24, 2016.
7. From Health Canada reports.

9: Comparisons

1. Statistic from Nishnawbe-Aski Police annual report 2010–2011.
2. Harold Cardinal, *The Unjust Society* (Vancouver: Douglas & McIntyre, 1999), 53.
3. Harold Cardinal, *The Unjust Society*, 12.
4. Ronet Bachman, *Death and Violence on the Reservation: Homicide, Family Violence, and Suicide in American Indian Populations*, (Westport, CT: Greenwood Publishing, 1992).
5. Louise Elliott, "Ontario native suicide rate one of the highest in the world, expert says," Canadian Press, November 27, 2000.
6. Ibid.
7. Information from 2010 Statistics Canada, median total income by Aboriginal identity, population aged 25–54.
8. Sari Horwitz, "The hard lives — and high suicide rate — of Native American children on reservations," *The Washington Post*, March 9, 2014.
9. United States Census Bureau, 2010 American Community Survey for the American Indian and Alaska Native alone population.
10. Anne Kazak et al., "A Social Rank Explanation of How Money Influences Health." *Journal of Health Psychology* 34, no. 3 (March 2015): 222–30.
11. PAC, RG 10, Vol. 3212, File 527, 787-4 Indian Agent J.P. Wright to D.C. Scott, December 20, 1919. The International Workers of the World (IWW) and One Big Union (OBU) were important socialist movements at the time.
12. PAC, RG 10, Vol. 3212, File 527, 787-4, Indian Agent McDonald to W.M. Graham, January 13, 1921.

10: When the Waters Rush In

1. Quoted in Hugh Shewell, *"Enough to Keep Them Alive": Indian Welfare in Canada, 1873–1965* (Toronto: University of Toronto Press, 2004), 228.
2. Éric Dewailly and Evert Nieboer, "Exposure and Preliminary Health Assessments of the Oujé-Bougomou Cree Population to Mine

Tailing Residues," Institut Montreal: National de Santé Publique du Québec, 2005.

3. See Chapter 11, "Relocation of Aboriginal Communities," in *RCAP, Volume 1, Looking Forward Looking Back*. See also, Cynthia Wesley-Esquimaux and Magdalena Smolewski, "Historic Trauma and Aboriginal Healing," Aboriginal Healing Foundation, 2004.

4. When asked to rate how stressful a forced relocation was compared to other life events, indigenous persons have consistently ranked the relocation as more damaging than anything else imaginable. In the 1988 journal of *American Indian and Alaska Native Mental Health Research*, Volume 2, no. 1: 3–19, researchers Michael J. O'Sullivan and Paul Handal asked the American Indian Yavapai community located near Phoenix, Arizona, how they felt about the possibility of relocation if a nearby dam at Fort McDowell was built. (The dam was first proposed in 1968, and had been on the cards ever since.) Even the threat of dispossession was far worse than any other conceivable tragedy. It was more upsetting than "death of a close family member, death of a close friend, major personal injury or illness, major change in health of family member, children leaving the reservation, divorce or marital separation, trouble with law or jail term." Below are the mean ratings of typical life-stresses compared to relocation for the Fort McDowell Community:

Death of close friend	64
Death of close family member	63
Major personal injury or illness	45
Major change in health of family member	56
Children leaving the reservation	36
Divorce or marital separation	36
Trouble with law or jail term	46
Stress of effects of relocation	
On tribal people and culture	79
Survival of the tribe	79
Overall on you personally	79

Eager to find out how the stress of relocation affected people's physical health, they compared these answers to a culturally similar American Indian community, which for privacy reasons was not named. Compared to the control community, there were more doctor's visits by the Yavapais, although the researchers did not specify what sort of physical problems the stress was causing, and whether the medical problems were, like the people of Kash, related to anxiety and panic. See also the pivotal study, M. Y. H. Brave Heart and L. M. DeBruyn, "The American Indian holocaust: Healing historical unresolved grief," *American Indian and Alaska Native Mental Health Research* 8, no. 2 (1998): 60–82.

11: A Call for Help

1. Quoted in Colin Perkel, "First Nations in 'state of shock' as they declare public-health emergency," Canadian Press, February 24, 2016.

12: Moral Injury

1. Geoffrey York, *The Dispossessed: Life and Death in Native Canada*, 143.
2. Elizabeth Thomlinson, Nellie Erickson, and M. Cook, "Could This Be Your Community?" in *No Place for Violence: Canadian Aboriginal Alternative*, ed. Jocelyn Proulx and Sharon Perrault (Halifax, NS: Fernwood Publishing, 2000).
3. Michael Bopp, Judie Bopp, and Phil Lane, "Aboriginal Domestic Violence in Canada," Aboriginal Healing Foundation, 2003.
4. L. Lix et al., "Risk Factors and Chronic Conditions Among Aboriginal and Non-Aboriginal Populations," Statistics Canada, 2009.
5. Jonathan Shay, *Achilles in Vietnam: Combat Trauma and the Undoing of Character* (New York: Simon & Schuster, 1994), 20.

13: The Crisis

1. From 2011 study by the federal government. Of Canada's 633 reserves, 571 participated.
2. Several versions of this story were told to me. Some said this meeting happened on October 21. Others said that the river water was brought in jugs or that a single glass of it was offered by a local to Gilles St. Pierre, a representative from Health Canada, First Nations and Inuit Health branch, Timmins. That river water was given to government officials was confirmed by a transcript of the meeting and several sources, including Alfred Wesley and Cree elder William Sutherland. But whose idea it was and who was asked to drink the water still remains unclear.
3. From a transcript given to me by Kashechewan teacher Carol Laronde.
4. In a July 2011 Health Canada study, 127 First Nations were on boil water advisories.
5. Richard Brennan and Robert Benzie, "Deadly E-coli threatens natives government must act, says Martin; 2,000 on reserve need vaccinations governments argue over responsibility," *Toronto Star*, October 25, 2005.
6. Julius Strauss, "Escape from Kashechewan: Those most affected by northern reserves tainted water head south," *Globe and Mail*, October 28, 2005.
7. Staff, "Troops saw Kashechewan operation as PR exercise," Canadian Press, May 14, 2006.
8. Murray Campbell, "Indifference to native people shows again; children sickened by contaminated water; federal government drenched in blame," *Globe and Mail*, October 27, 2005.
9. Hansard Transcripts, Legislative Assembly of Ontario, October 26, 2005.

14: Where Next?

1. Harold Cardinal, *The Unjust Society,* 26.
2. Jonathan Lear, *Radical Hope: Ethics in the Face of Cultural Devastation* (Cambridge, MA: Harvard University Press, 2006).
3. Jeffrey Simpson, "Canada's great First Nations experiment," *Globe and Mail*, July 30, 2014.

Acknowledgements

There are many, many people who went out of their way to make this book a reality. Here is a taxonomy of acknowledgements:

Research: Andrew Reuben for his historical, linguistic, and cultural knowledge; Julie Wesley, for her endless help; Jesse McCormick for his legal expertise; reporter Connie Walker for her many insights; Chief Shining Turtle (English name Franklin Paibomsai) of the Whitefish River First Nation; Andrew Wesley for helping me understand the Cree traditions; poet and playwright Tomson Highway; Arthur Schwartzel for his help navigating CBC video resources; Reverend Travis Enright; Fan Brunning; Jenny Lewis, for her contextual insights; Cynthia Wesley-Esquimaux, for her expertise on the residential schools; Dr. Lindsay MacMillan; Rob Clarke, former MP for Desnethé — Missinippi — Churchill River; Wayne Spear; author Hans Carlson for the history of James Bay area; professor and author Hugh Shewell for his historical and political knowledge; Guy Ginter for helping me understand Impact Benefit Agreements.

Editorial: My brilliant editor Michael Melgaard, copyeditor Dilia Narduzzi, editorial director Carrie Gleason, acquiring editor Diane Young, managing editor Kathryn Lane, publisher Kirk Howard, and my agents Chris Casuccio and John Pearce.

Financial: Thanks to Toronto Arts Council, Ontario Arts Council, and Canada Council for the Arts for generously supporting me in the research and writing of this book.

Personal: My parents Ailsa, Jonathan, Steven, and Eva, my brothers and sisters Augusta, Sidonie, Tim, and Danielle; Jill Grove, Elaine Wong, John Krizanc, Eve Joseph, Amanda Lewis, Diane Martin, Barbara Gowdy, Mary Albino, Andrew Micak, Patricia Pearson, Joss Maclennan, Michael Schellenberg, Danielle Boily, Steven Friedman, Tali Boritz, Andrea Carson Barker, Lorna Vallings, Dianne de Fenoyl, Jeff Warren, Sarah Barmak, and for her endless patience, love, and wisdom, my partner Lia Grimanis.

And finally to the people of Kashechewan: For letting me stay, and giving me an important lesson in determination, courage, and resilience.

VISIT US AT

Dundurn.com
@dundurnpress
Facebook.com/dundurnpress
Pinterest.com/dundurnpress